Especially for

_____

From

_____

Date

_____

On My Way

Home

Devotions Inspired
by the Beloved Classic
Stepping Heavenward

BARBOUR

© 2014 by Barbour Publishing, Inc.

Print ISBN 978-1-62416-860-4

eBook Editions:
Adobe Digital Edition (.epub) 978-1-63058-103-9
Kindle and MobiPocket Edition (.prc) 978-1-63058-104-6

Devotional writing by Angie Kiesling in association with Snapdragon Group℠.

Published by Barbour Publishing, Inc., P.O. Box 719, Uhrichsville, Ohio 44683,
www.barbourbooks.com

Our mission is to publish and distribute inspirational products offering exceptional value and biblical encouragement to the masses.

Member of the
Evangelical Christian
Publishers Association

Printed in the United States of America.

Introduction

Described as the story of a woman's journey to godliness, *Stepping Heavenward* by Elizabeth Prentiss stands out as a spiritual classic because of its unique format: the fictional account of a young woman named Katherine Mortimer written in the form of a journal kept by Katherine herself. Its memorable opening words give us a peek into the delightful chronicle that awaits: "How dreadfully old I am getting! Sixteen! Well, I don't see as I can help it. There it is in the big Bible in Father's own hand."

But what really makes Prentiss's book so special is the fact that Katherine is not portrayed as a Pollyanna saint with only godly thoughts and actions—a characterization approach widely used in the mid-nineteenth century. Instead she leaps off the page with all the foibles and blunt speech and character flaws of any real-world person. Like any young woman struggling to grow up in both life and faith, Katherine wrestles with her unruly nature, falls in and out of love, questions her salvation, and demands answers from a God who sometimes seems silent and distant. The story of her growth, as shown through the journal entries, offers a glimpse into the "heavenward" progression of a woman as real as any of us today—proving that the enduring qualities of faith and character are indeed truly timeless.

The pages ahead provide a look into Prentiss's amazing volume, with a simple excerpt, accompanied by a contemporary devotional designed to strike a chord in the heart of today's reader. We pray that as you read you will be blessed by the message as captured by two writers of similar faith but different eras.

To every thing there is a season,
and a time to every purpose under the heaven.

ECCLESIASTES 3:1 KJV

Talking to God

*"I hurried off, and just as I got to the door of the schoolroom,
it flashed into my mind that I had not said my prayers! A nice way
to begin on one's birthday to be sure! Well, I had no time. And perhaps
my good resolutions pleased God almost as much as one of my rambling
stupid prayers could. For I must admit I can't make good prayers.
I can't think of anything to say. I often wonder what Mother finds
to say when she is shut up by the hour praying."*

Mommy, can I show you something?" a child asks,
clutching a folded manila paper to her chest.

"Not now, sweetie. Mommy's busy," her mother replies
as she types an e-mail, missing the cloud that passes over her
daughter's face.

Later that afternoon, on an errand run, the little girl calls
from her place in the backseat of the car, "Mommy, can you
look at my picture now?" But her question is interrupted by her
mother's cell phone ringing.

"Mommy, can you see what I made you now?" the little girl
asks during dinner that evening.

"Of course," her mom responds brightly. "Just let me
get these dishes washed, and I'll come to your room." Three
hours pass and suddenly it's bedtime for her daughter. *Ah*, the

mother thinks, *I remembered—before the day is past.* Tucking in her daughter, she says, "Now what did you have to show me?"

The little girl blinks, her eyes heavy with sleep. "I put it on your chair."

Back at her desk, the mother finds the folded paper on the seat of her computer chair. Inside is a picture of a house and two smiling stick figures—one big, one little—and the words "Best mommy in the world" scrawled in a childish hand.

How easy it is to forget to talk to God in the bluster and busyness of our days. Taking time for prayer seems like just one more thing on our to-do list—an item that can easily get crossed off in favor of more pressing matters. After all, we reason, how do our feeble words help God out? Do our "rambling stupid prayers" really matter in the great scheme of things?

They matter more than we may ever know. God longs to hear from us, and He longs to tell us what's on His heart. When we quiet ourselves, we are able to hear His still, small voice whisper, "Can I show you something?"

The prayer of the upright is [God's] delight.
PROVERBS 15:8 KJV

A Useful Woman

*"Mother [said] that I had in me the elements of a fine character if I
would only conquer some of my faults. 'You are frank and truthful,'
she said, 'and in some things conscientious. I hope you are really
a child of God and are trying to please Him. And it is my daily
prayer that you may become a lovely, loving, useful woman.'"*

Another nineteenth-century author had a high regard for being "useful"—a term that sounds strange to our twenty-first-century ears. Wouldn't we rather be called attractive. . .or kind. . .or loving. . .or productive. . .or successful? *Useful?* What a dull, utilitarian word it seems. Perhaps the secret to true usefulness eludes us.

The author provides a clue. In a letter to her sister about a favorite niece, Jane Austen writes: "We thought of and talked of her yesterday. . .and wished her a long enjoyment of all the happiness to which she seems born. While she gives happiness to those about her, she is pretty sure of her own share."

Usefulness *is* love and kindness in action, seeing what people need and helping them to get it—even if it means putting ourselves to some trouble or stepping outside our comfort zones. The same writer also believed that "wisdom is better than wit" (though she wielded a razor-sharp wit herself) and that *goodness* trumps beauty and superficial charm every time.

She lets her characters do the talking. In a scene from their childhood, the hero of *Mansfield Park* is trying to comfort the heroine, who has just relocated to strange new surroundings—far from her immediate family—and spends every night crying herself to sleep. "And sitting down by her, he was at great pains to overcome her shame. . .and persuade her to speak openly. . . . 'Let us walk out in the park, [he said] and you shall tell me all about your brothers and sisters.'"

One of the greatest kindnesses of all, it turns out, is simply listening to those around us—seeing them for who they really are and letting them tell their "stories." The "elements of a fine character"—being frank and truthful and conscientious and pleasing to God—are, in the end, the very essence of being a "lovely, loving, useful" man or woman.

> *There are different kinds of service,*
> *but the same Lord.*
> 1 CORINTHIANS 12:5

More Than a Pretty Book

"On the table, by the window, I saw a beautiful new desk in place of the old clumsy thing I had been spattering and spoiling so many years. A little note, full of love, said it was from Mother and begged me every day of my life to read and reflect upon a few verses of a tastefully bound copy of the Bible that accompanied the desk."

That particular Christmas would always be remembered for more than the snow that fell, turning the landscape wintry white, and for more than the surprises that turned up under the tree. Instead, it would become a bookmark in her life, a turning point on her spiritual path—the day she received a Bible inscribed by her mother, two months after her thirteenth birthday.

The padded green leather Bible, embossed with gold letters, felt weighty and solid in her hands. She ran her fingers over the cover, feeling the tiny grooves where the letters indented the leather. She inhaled its rich scent.

"Hey, whatcha got there?" her brother blurted, snatching the gift out of her hands.

"No! Give it back!" She tried to wrest the precious book from her brother's hands, but he was too quick.

He frowned. "A stupid book. . .a Bible? Wow, I'm jealous."

He tossed the Bible on the floor and turned his attention back to his new bicycle.

He couldn't know what the Bible meant to her. As she picked it up and lovingly brushed off its cover, she thought of the night a few months earlier when she had knelt by her bed and spoken to God one-on-one for the first time. She had given her heart to Him, and her mother must have realized it was time for a "grown-up Bible."

She left the hubbub in the living room—shredded wrapping paper flying everywhere, her four siblings chattering about their presents—and found a quiet corner in the bedroom she shared with her sister. Opening the Bible, she saw her mother's handwriting, dedicating the Bible to her and ending with a verse that would become "her" scripture.

If we delight ourselves in the Lord, as the psalmist wrote, the Bible will become so much more than just a collection of ancient stories and rituals. To the contrary, we will discover that every word is "God-breathed," as the apostle Paul said, and alive with meaning and direction for every step of our lives.

All Scripture is inspired by God and is useful for teaching,
for showing people what is wrong in their lives,
for correcting faults, and for teaching how to live right.
2 Timothy 3:16 ncv

Bargaining with God

"I opened the Bible at random and lighted on these words: 'Watch therefore: for ye know not what hour your Lord doth come' (Matthew 24:42). There was nothing very cheering in that. . . . I am sure I am not fit to die. Besides, I want to have a good time with nothing to worry me. I hope I shall live ever so long. Perhaps in the course of forty or fifty years I may get tired of this world and want to leave it. And I hope by that time I shall be a great deal better than I am now and fit to go to heaven."

He paddled out farther than he had intended, feeling the surf lift and carry him even farther still. Glancing back at the shoreline, he gauged his distance and reminded himself that he was a strong swimmer. But after a few minutes of paddling, he was no closer to the shore than when he started. A scary realization crept into his mind—he was caught in the riptide.

He sent up a desperate plea: *God, help me!* He remembered the times God had been there for him throughout his life, faithful even in the little things. When he nearly lost his faith as a child, God spoke to him through a rainbow. *God, help me!* When his beloved grandmother died, the Lord held him close. *God, help me!* When he got laid off from his job and foreclosed on the mortgage, God helped him rebuild his family's life one day at a time.

"God, help me!" he sputtered as he thrashed in the water. And in that instant he remembered a bit of wisdom learned in childhood, words that came to him as a thought not his own: *Swim along the shoreline, not toward the shore.* Of course!

He gulped a lungful of air and let the current lift and carry him, then used his arms to swim parallel to the shore, gradually edging closer and closer until his feet touched ground and he waded up onto the sand and collapsed.

None of us knows the number of days allotted to us, but we can trust our "life and times" to the God who has numbered the very hairs of our heads. In that place of abiding trust, we also are assured that nothing—absolutely nothing—can snatch us out of this life and into the presence of God until He decides it is time.

"Even the hairs of your head are all counted.
Do not be afraid; you are of more value than many sparrows."

LUKE 12:7 NRSV

"It is more than a month since I took that cold, and here I still am, shut up in the house. To be sure the doctor lets me go downstairs, but then he won't listen to a word about school. Oh, dear! All the girls will get ahead of me. This is Sunday, and everybody has gone to church. . . . I am sure I pray to God to make me better, and why doesn't He?"

She wasn't supposed to know, but she did—her best friend was planning a surprise birthday party for her, and it promised to be the most memorable day of her life. She couldn't help it that she'd overheard the phone conversation, so she held her tongue and determined to act surprised.

Her friend was coy, saying, "Why don't I take you antique browsing on your birthday. And then lunch at one of those cozy little tearooms on Antique Row?" Smiling a secret smile, she agreed—knowing this was just a ruse to get her to the real party location.

But as the weeks flew by and the big day drew near, an unwelcome visitor came calling: the dreaded flu bug that was going through town. Lying in bed, she reached for another tissue and counted the days in her mind: only two to go till her birthday.

The next two days passed in a blur of fever and flu

wretchedness. Her prayer partner called and prayed for her (but nothing happened). Her mom came by and spoon-fed her liquids and chicken noodle soup. Was God ignoring her prayers?

Her birthday dawned overcast and raining. *Good,* she thought. *Just how I feel, and now the party can't happen anyway.*

But she was wrong. At two o'clock in the afternoon, the doorbell rang and her best friend came into her room, smiling from ear to ear. "Let's get you into a nice clean robe and prop you up against some pillows." And she did so just in time, because over the next hour friend after friend dropped by, forming a steady stream of birthday well-wishers at the bedroom door. They came bearing flowers, cards, gifts, and smiles.

When the last person had left and she was all alone with her thoughts again, she thanked God for the very *welcome visitors* that came calling that day.

God may answer our prayers—for comfort, for companionship, for healing—in ways we never expected, but we can be assured He will answer. . .in His time, in His way.

[God] does not ignore the cries of the afflicted.

PSALM 9:12

God's Goodness, Not Ours

"I hate to own it to myself and to write it down here, but I will. I do not love to pray. I am always eager to get it over with and out of the way so as to have leisure to enjoy myself. I mean that this is usually so. This morning I cried a good deal while I was on my knees and felt sorry for my quick temper and all my bad ways. If I always felt so, perhaps praying would not be such a task. I wish I knew whether anybody exactly as bad as I am ever got to heaven at last? I have read ever so many memoirs, and they were all about people who were too good to live, and so died, or else went on a mission; I am not at all like any of them."

It is a miracle of the Christian faith that any of us makes it into heaven at all—but, thank God, we do! Think about it: nobody has to teach a toddler how to throw a tantrum or pull her playmate's hair; those tendencies toward "badness" are already there, a built-in part of our human nature even from babyhood. And we only get worse with the passage of years.

Somebody swerves into the parking space we're waiting for—we lean on the horn and swear a blue streak. A colleague gets the promotion that should have been ours—we fume in private envy and stew over unkind thoughts. The panhandler on the corner gets uncomfortably close to our car—we zoom past him as soon as the light turns green, refusing eye contact.

We may look good on the outside, but the inside can get pretty ugly at times.

God saw the situation, saw how far short of hitting the mark we were, and decided to do something about it. Jesus did what we fallible humans could never do. He offered to exchange our "badness" for His "goodness" by paying the ultimate price—His life. Our part is simply to believe in Him.

If we dig deep enough into the lives of the "spiritual giants" of history, we'll find they were every bit as flawed— every bit as *human*—as we are. Yet what does God do? He writes them on the palm of His hand and makes an everlasting agreement to be their God. He promises to be our God, too, if only we will say yes to Jesus.

> *[God] made Him who knew no sin to be sin on our behalf,*
> *so that we might become the righteousness of God in Him.*

2 CORINTHIANS 5:21 NASB

A Beeline for the Belfry

*"Dear Mother! I wonder how I can ever forget what troubles
she has had, and am not always sweet and loving. She has gone
now, where she always goes when she feels sad, straight to God.
Of course she did not say so, but I know Mother."*

A monk from another century found a special way to deal
with his downcast moments, those times when "what troubles
he had" weighed too heavy for him to cope with alone. Instead
of closing himself in his cell to pray, he made a beeline for the
belfry.

High up in the monastery's bell tower, he could be alone
with God—alone with his thoughts—and gaze out over the
mountain landscape. Spilling his troubles out loud to his Lord,
he would grab hold of the belfry rope and swing away, up
and down, up and down, as the bells rang out the tune of his
remorse followed by swift-coming relief.

The other monks in the monastery always knew when their
brother had to "deal with God," as he called it. At those odd
hours when the belfry should have remained silent, they would
hear its bell pealing out across the countryside. And soon their
brother monk would return to them at peace, a soft smile on
his face.

Where do we go when the troubles of life pile up too high and the weight of it is more than we can bear? Do we grumble and complain, adding to our woes by the words of our mouth? Do we simmer in stoic silence, teaching ourselves to "grin and bear it" until the troubles pass by? Do we heap our problems at our friends' feet, hoping they can somehow find us a loophole of mercy? Or do we go straight to God?

Each of us has to find the place where we can best meet with our Father. For some it's a walk out in nature, where every blade of grass declares the wonder of our Maker. For others it may be a quiet corner of a room, with the door closed. Some may find God in the crash of waves on the shore or looking up at the craggy peaks pointing heavenward. The place doesn't matter. What matters is that we go straight to our God, the One who wants to take our worries upon Himself.

Cast your cares on the LORD and he will sustain you;
he will never let the righteous be shaken.

PSALM 55:22

Incessant Prayer

"'My dear Katy,' [Mother] said, 'I wish I could make you see that God is just as willing and just as able to sanctify as He is to redeem us. It would save you so much weary, disappointing work. But God has opened my eyes at last.' 'I wish He would open mine, then,' I said, 'for all I see now is that I am just as horrid as I can be and that the more I pray the worse I grow.' 'That is not true, dear,' she replied. 'Go on praying—pray without ceasing.'"

Flinging off her slippers, she walked to the window facing the backyard and the woods beyond and opened it wide. The pink light of dusk settled over everything, coloring the world with a rosy hue that quickly turned dark purple as nightfall set in. It had been a rough day—too rough. The kind of day everyone wants to forget.

A breeze rustled the trees and blew in the window. As she inhaled deeply, she realized she had a choice. She could either replay the day's events in her mind incessantly, wallowing in wretchedness, or stop and invite God into her troubles. Right now. This very moment.

Unintentionally, she started to contemplate the day's problems then caught herself, making the wise choice. Breathing in the cool night air, she asked God to deal with each trouble in His timing, in His way.

As God-seekers, we, too, will face moment-by-moment choices, and the right choice—the wise choice—is always as plain as the noses on our faces. No matter what troubles us, we take it to our Father and drop it at His feet.

Oh, He won't be offended. . . . He actually *asks* us to do this. Our willingness to "let go and let God" is the highest mark of devotion in His eyes. There's even an old-fashioned (and unpopular) word for it: obedience.

"Pray without ceasing," a long-ago saint wrote. But we wonder: How on earth can we pray every minute of every day? How do we really pray incessantly?

The answer is as simple as breathing—spiritual breathing, in fact. As we go about our days and nights, through our joys and sorrows, our victories and defeats, we talk to God in a running dialogue of spirit and mind.

Rejoice always, pray without ceasing.

1 Thessalonians 5:16–17 nrsv

Too Much to Ask?

"'I do wish I could make you love to pray, my darling child,' Mother went on. 'If you only knew the strength, and the light, and the joy you might have for the simple asking. God attaches no conditions to His gifts. He only says, "Ask!"'" This may be true, but it is hard work to pray. It tires me. And I do wish there was some easy way of growing good. In fact, I should like to have God send a sweet temper to me just as He sent bread and meat to Elijah. I don't believe Elijah had to kneel down and pray for them."

If we were God, we'd soon grow tired of all the prayers thrown up to heaven. *Can't those foolish humans figure it out by now?* But we're not God (thank God!). If we were God, we'd put a statute of limitations on "prayer laundry lists." *You're wearing Me out with your constant needs!* But we're not.

If we were God, we'd wonder how many answered prayers it takes for our faith to gain traction. *Did you already forget what I did for you the last time. . . ?* But we're not God (thank God!). If we were God, we'd get our fill of dealing with petulance and bad tempers. But we're not.

As He provided bread and meat to His prophet, the Lord is ready to provide for our every need—not just when we ask, but even before we ask. God deals in the unexpected, the extraordinary, and the easily missed (if we don't have eyes to see and recognize His good gifts). And they're always truly good gifts, even though they're not always what we *expected.*

Imagine if the prophet had begged God for food as he hid out by the brook, then shooed the ravens away when they tried to land near him. It's like the story of the flood victim who prays for God to rescue him, then sits tight while he waits for his miracle. Three different times he turns down help because he's waiting for a spectacular display of God's might. When the floodwaters rise and he cries out, "Lord, why didn't You save me?" God answers: *"But I sent help to you three times, and all three times you refused it."*

Whatever our crisis or need or desire, if we simply ask according to His will, He is quick to answer it.

This is the confidence we have in approaching God:
that if we ask anything according to his will, he hears us.

1 John 5:14

Seeds of Promise

⟋⟋⟍⟍

"Last Sunday Dr. Cabot preached to the young. He first addressed those who knew they did not love God. It did not seem to me that I belonged to that class. Then he spoke to those who knew they did. I felt sure I was not one of those. Last of all he spoke affectionately to those who did not know what to think, and I was frightened and ashamed to feel tears running down my cheeks when he said that he believed that most of his hearers who were in this doubtful state did really love their Master, only their love was something as new and as tender and perhaps as unobserved as the tiny point of green that, forcing its way through the earth, is yet unconscious of its own existence but promises a thrifty plant."

The miracle of a seed is that all the vibrant possibility of life is encased within one tiny promise of the tree or vine or vegetable or flower to come. All it needs is good soil, a little sunshine, and water. And so it is with our hearts.

Dirt comes in all types: sandy, rocky, thorny. . .or the rich black soil that is so valuable it gets bagged and sold at gardening shops. Gardeners who live in sandy climates know they need to add potting soil to make their plants and flowers grow.

Gardeners who live in rocky terrains must rid the ground of rocks if they want a successful garden. The same goes for gardeners working on a patch of land riddled with thorns. If they don't pull up the thorns, the prickly weeds and vines will choke out any new life. But the gardener fortunate enough to work with soil that is rich and black and moist knows his soil is just right.

Our hearts may warm to a message about God, but we soon forget it or get carried away by the issues of the day. Or perhaps we cry and make promises to "live right"—really meaning it—but we just can't seem to stay the course. We may even find ourselves in a place where we're angry at God and want nothing to do with Him, our hearts embittered by disappointment or suffering or loss. But maybe, just maybe, when the words of God fall on our ears, they go down into our hearts and find a nesting place, just like a seed that is pushed down into good soil.

> *[Jesus said to them,] "Others, like seed sown on good soil, hear the word, accept it, and produce a crop—some thirty, some sixty, some a hundred times what was sown."*

MARK 4:20

Unreasonable Love

"'You cannot prove to yourself that you love God by examining your feelings toward Him. They are indefinite and they fluctuate. But just as far as you obey Him, just so far, depend upon it, you love Him. It is not natural to us sinful, ungrateful human beings to prefer His pleasure to our own or to follow His way instead of our own way, and nothing, nothing but love of Him can or does make us obedient to Him.'"

A young woman arrives at a park on a summer's day, shades her eyes with her hand, and looks out over the clusters of people dotting the landscape. She knows he is here; he said he would be—and he always keeps his word to her. Scanning the park, her eyes finally light on a lone figure standing straight and tall against an oak tree, nearly hidden from view by the leafy curtain. Gazing right at her, the figure lifts one hand in a wave. . . . It's him. A smile breaks across her face as the young woman shifts her picnic basket and heads toward the tree, toward him. He starts walking out to meet her and catches her in his arms.

In a crowd of people, it's easy to pick out the ones in love— we see them gazing at each other, laughing and holding hands, flirting playfully, or running to do some small errand for the object of their affection. Whether it's romantic love, friendship love, or familial love—such as the love of a mother for her child—the presence of *love* is hard to miss.

Love is the strongest motivator to action, and when we love someone we are happiest when we make them happy in return. That's what God had in mind when He created us with a free will and the right to choose whether to love Him back. He didn't want a bunch of robots for His most beloved creation, humans. No, He desired to love and *be loved* by us in return. He is the author of authentic, passionate, *unreasonable* love, the kind that gives simply for the joy of giving, not giving to get. The only proof of true love is if it is reciprocated. And if it's not, we question whether love ever existed for that person.

Following after God goes against the current of our culture, yet we rush headlong to do it—boldly proclaiming our kinship with Him—if we truly love Him.

Jesus replied: "Love the Lord your God with all your heart and with all your soul and with all your mind."

MATTHEW 22:37

Walking the Line

"Amelia has been here. She has had another talk with Dr. Cabot
and is perfectly happy. She says it is so easy to be a Christian!
It may be easy for her; everything is. She never has any of my dreadful
feelings and does not understand them when I try to explain them to her.
Well! If I am fated to be miserable, I must try to bear it."

Choosing to walk the "straight and narrow"—the way of
Christ—is not something to take lightly, yet many people
pitch Christianity the way they would an item at a garage sale.
They want to make a "quick sale" and get another notch in
their soul-winning belt, so they portray a life full of favor and
blessings backed up by eternal fire insurance (with a get-out-of-
hell-free card).

Yes, following Christ comes with joy and favor and
blessings, but we would be wise to remember the flipside of the
coin: Jesus Himself warned us that in this world we will endure
trials of various kinds, face persecution for our belief in Him,
and often end up last rather than first. And after we "suffer a
little while," we get to go to heaven. Wait—this wasn't what we
signed up for!

Yes, we are told to "count the cost" before signing on
the dotted line, for the price is indeed high—very high. No

doubt Christianity fills us with joy, but it might make us a little miserable along the way, while our character is being pounded and shaped on the Potter's wheel.

We, too, may feel as if we are "fated to be miserable" at times, but as we continue to head in the direction of Christ, following His footsteps, we will discover what it truly means to be alive in Him.

When describing the Christian life, a first-century prophet wrote about "joy unspeakable and full of glory." His own life path was no cakewalk. He endured much, suffered much, hoped much, but his faith was rewarded with a life of meaning and adventure that will have eternal ramifications. Looking down from heaven, we can be assured he wouldn't trade his choice to walk the line for anything in this world. What about us? Are we ready to do whatever God asks of us, whether that something is comfortable or not?

My comfort in my suffering is this:
Your promise preserves my life.

PSALM 119:50

Battlefield Behavior

"When soldiers drop wounded on the battlefield, they are taken up tenderly and carried 'to the rear,' which means, I suppose, out of sight and sound. Is anybody mad enough to suppose it will do them any good to hear Scripture quoted—sermons launched at them before their open, bleeding wounds are staunched? Mother assents, in a mild way, when I talk so and says, 'Yes, yes, we are indeed lying wounded on the battlefield of life and in no condition to listen to any words save those of pity. But, dear Katy, we must interpret aright all the well meant attempts of our friends to comfort us. They mean sympathy, however awkwardly they express it.'"

There's a scene in the classic film *Gone with the Wind* that's shocking no matter how many times we see it. As Scarlett rushes to find a doctor to help her friend give birth during wartime, she stumbles into the enormous open-air "hospital" at the city's railroad depot. What greets her eyes—and ours— is unforgettable.

As the camera slowly pulls back, it shows a panoramic view of thousands of wounded and dead soldiers lying in the hot sun. We hear the wails of the men in pain, and silence from those who have died. The movie director makes sure we get the point: the ravages of war, up close and personal, are horrifying.

It's been said that Christianity is the only army that shoots its wounded. Instead of nursing those who trip and fall back to health, we often attack them while they're down, firing hurtful words at them instead of offering the balm of kindness. Oh, we may do it with a smile on our faces, or pepper our words with scripture quotes to help our fellow soldiers. But is the end result healing or hurting?

God means business when He tells us to "tame the tongue" (James 3:8), for in it lies the "power of life and death" (Proverbs 18:21). And remember that childhood rhyming chant "Sticks and stones may break my bones, but words can never hurt me"? Well, it doesn't take long for us as children. . .as teenagers. . .as adults to realize the very opposite is true. Words hurt *more* than any blunt force against our bodies. Words have the power to heal or wound the soul for a person's natural lifetime.

As we step among the wounded who have fallen, what is our battlefield behavior? Will we choose words of healing or words that injure?

> *When you talk, do not say harmful things. But say what people need—words that will help others become stronger.*
>
> EPHESIANS 4:29 ICB

A Place of Contentment

"My school days are over! I have come off with flying colors, and Mother is pleased at my success. I said to her today that I should now have time to draw and practice to my heart's content. 'You will not find your heart content with either,' she said. 'Why, Mother!' I cried, 'I thought you liked to see me happy!' 'And so I do,' she said quietly. 'But there is something better to get out of life than you have yet found.' 'I am sure I hope so,' I returned. On the whole I haven't got much so far."

At every stage of life, we seem to strain to reach some distant goal—and when we reach it, we know we will be happy. At last we will find our heart's content. When we're children, all we want to do is grow up. When we're teenagers, we just can't wait to drive—yes, *that's* when our life will truly begin. And when we're in our twenties, we can't wait to finish college or get married or have children (insert goal here).

Of course, when we finally get the job of our dreams, we look forward to being promoted. And, oh, what a joy it will be when we can retire and no longer have to *go* to that job every day! But if we were free to play all day, we would quickly grow bored. Why? Because God made us to work, and more to the point, He made us to work for Him. He created us with an inborn desire to have purpose and find meaning in what we do.

And all our significance—our truest heart's content—can only be found in Him.

No wonder the twelve apostles "turned the world upside down" at the cost of their own lives. No wonder they left their fishing nets and tax-collecting jobs to follow after the One who promised to take them on the adventure of their lives. They were fired up from within by the very creative life-spark of God. Everything else paled in comparison to that high calling.

And so it is with us. Apart from God, apart from the purpose and destiny He has inscribed in our "book," we will be frustrated and discontented, wondering when our lives will begin and constantly asking, "Is this all there is to life?" Thankfully, the answer is no—there is so much more to life if we will but embrace it. . .if we will but embrace *Him.*

Walk worthy of the Lord unto all pleasing, being fruitful in every good work, and increasing in the knowledge of God.

COLOSSIANS 1:10 KJV

Uneasy Words

"Dr. Cabot preaches as if we all had to die pretty soon or else have something almost as bad happen to us. How can old people always try to make young people feel uncomfortable and as if things couldn't last?"

$\mathcal{T}$he crowd had gathered on the hillside to hear the words of the itinerant preacher some said came straight from God. Incredulous, others whispered that He even claimed to be the Son of God.

Like any crowd, some jostled for the best seats on the ground and chattered loudly. Those with sick or disabled loved ones pushed their way to the front, having heard the stories about the preacher's ability to heal. Mothers corralled their children, ordering them to sit quietly as the preacher stood to His feet and started to speak.

Some of the preacher's words were just what they hoped to hear—words of blessing and goodness falling into their laps. Words about how much God loved them. But then the preacher's words took a left turn, making them uncomfortable, uneasy. Did God really expect so much of them? And what was it He said about how to treat their neighbors?

Yet somehow, in spite of their discomfort, they hung on the speaker's every word. He had a strange way about Him—not dryly reciting from the ancient texts but speaking as if He knew something they didn't. . .knew *Someone* they didn't.

Worst of all, His words forced them to make a choice. They could no longer claim ignorance. They could no longer pretend they didn't know the truth. The question was what would they do with that truth? Would they turn and head back home—content to settle for life as usual? Or would they sign on for the long haul, ready to be changed forever by the Son of God?

Each of us is confronted with the uncomfortable truth—God's truth—at some point in our lives. Like a divine schoolteacher, He sends people across our paths, plants billboards on our highways, drops flyers into our mailboxes, and generally sets about the task of *making us uncomfortable* with the truth of who He is.

It might take years, decades even, but God is patient, pursuing us with His love until we are forced to make a choice. What will we do with His truth?

> *Lead me in Your truth and teach me, for You are the*
> *God of my salvation; on You I wait all the day.*
>
> PSALM 25:5 NKJV

Even the Little Things

"Mother shut herself up and, I have no doubt, prayed over [my relationship with Charley]. I really believe she prays over every new dress she buys. Then she sent for me and talked beautifully, and I behaved abominably."

Every afternoon when the little girl got home from school, she ran to the cage that sat in the corner of her room to check on her furry friend—the spotted mouse she'd seen at the pet store. It was love at first sight. And now, many months later, she'd fallen into a routine of feeding her beloved pet and cleaning its cage, taking the tiny animal out to play with now and then. She knew the mouse would always be waiting for her when she got home from school—until suddenly it wasn't.

On this particular day, the girl ran to the cage and found it empty. The spotted mouse had somehow jiggled the gate open and escaped from the cage, disappearing into some nook or cranny—which most likely seemed very large when seen through the eyes of a small rodent.

The girl ran to her mother sobbing, her face streaked with hot tears. "Why don't we pray and ask God to return your mouse safely," her mother said. The girl nodded, unable to speak. Together they sat down and prayed. "Lord, You promise to take care of us in all our ways," said the mother, "and You care about the little things. . . . You even care about this mouse, who is so loved. We don't know where she is, Father, but You do. Please let us find her safe and sound."

The little girl had grown up hearing about God at home and in church. She knew He was a big God. Was it possible He truly cared about something as small as a mouse—for someone as small as she?

Later that evening, after dinner and homework were cleared away, the little girl went back to her room to get ready for bed. And there, curled up in a tiny ball, half hidden by the comforter, was her mouse, sleeping peacefully.

We think God only cares about the big things in our lives—who we date or marry, which job to take, sickness and calamity, how we treat ourselves and others—but He is so much "bigger" than that. So big in fact that He's careful even about the smallest details of our lives.

> *[Jesus said,] "Whatsoever ye shall ask the Father in my name, he will give it you."*
>
> JOHN 16:23 KJV

Nursed by Love

"Poor Mother is dreadfully anxious about me. But I don't see
how she can love me so after the way I have behaved. I wonder if,
after all, mothers are not the best friends there are! I keep her
awake with my cough all night and am mopey and cross all day,
but she is just as kind and affectionate as she can be."

There's nothing like being sick or stressed to test our character.
While things are on an even keel, we're all sunshine and smiles,
a poster child for the goodness of God. But let us get knocked
flat with illness, or stretched to our limits by stress, and our true
colors come pouring out like paints spilled onto a canvas.

"Character is the way you act when no one is watching"
the old saying goes, and we feel the truth of those words
keenly when we suddenly "act" contrary to everything good
we thought about ourselves. Are we not kind? Are we not long-
suffering and gracious? Are we not forgiving and forbearing?
Are we loving and gentle? Ah, no. . .not half as much as we
thought we were.

Of all the tests God puts us through in life, one of the
most difficult is how we spend the "mundane hours," as one
great spiritual thinker termed it. What do we do when life gets
tedious and the people around us get on our last nerve? What

are we like when the days plod by with no discernible meaning beyond the routine of ordinariness?

We thought we signed on for some grand adventure, yet we slog through our days and nights feeling trapped in mediocrity. Where is the excitement we dreamed of when we said yes to God? Where is the life we thought would be ours?

Like the karate kid, we have great expectations and go to our Lord to be taught His ways—yet find ourselves doing menial chores, "wax on, wax off. . .wax on, wax off," never dreaming that through those ordinary disciplines our wise Teacher is training us for greatness.

When we, too, are "mopey and cross" all day, God is good enough to rain down His kindness and love and forbearance on us, often in ways we least expected. He is rewarded when at last we come to our senses and thank Him for His goodness.

Endurance produces character,
and character produces hope.

ROMANS 5:4 NRSV

At Arm's Length

"The day I wrote that was Sunday. I could not go to church, and I felt very forlorn and desolate. I tried to get some comfort by praying; but when I got on my knees, I just burst out crying and could not say a word."

God is a gentleman and never forces us into His presence. If we're feeling distant—far from our Father—it's not He who moved. Like the wheel of a ship set one degree off course, we may be miles out at sea before we realize our error. And by then it takes a dramatic effort to get us back on course and heading in the right direction.

A young man made a brilliant start with God, his heart seized with all the wonder and promise of the Gospel. He packed his new life with virtuous activities and hung out with like-minded believers. There was an obvious change in his life.

But one day he got invited to a rock concert with some old buddies from his garage band days. Why not, he figured. A little live music wouldn't hurt. After that night, his old friends urged him to start a new band with them—he played a mean guitar, they said, and he missed the camaraderie of music and laughter.

The next week when his Bible study group rolled around, he had to miss it because the band wanted to rehearse that night. It was just one night. . .no biggie. He could always go the following week. And of course he got home so late from the new Saturday night gigs that he started missing church on Sunday mornings. He meant well, of course, and God knew his heart.

After a couple of months he realized he'd made it to church only once or twice in the past several weeks. He stopped calling his believer friends because, well, he was just so busy with the band. Still, a recurring thought nagged at him in the quiet hours: his awareness of God had grown slightly dimmer, and he wondered why.

No matter how far away we drift, God never loses sight of us. When we ask, He gently and lovingly pulls us back on course. He loves us that much, and He's always quick to forgive. It could be said that the Christian life is *mostly* about course corrections.

> *My sacrifice, O God, is a broken spirit; a broken*
> *and contrite heart you, God, will not despise.*
>
> PSALM 51:17

God's Storage Attic

"[Mother] burst into tears and opened her arms, and I ran into them as a wounded bird flies into the ark. We cried together. Mother never said, never looked, 'I told you so.' All she did say was this: 'God has heard my prayers! He is reserving better things for my child!'"

Like children on a treasure hunt at a rambling country house, we can't imagine what our heavenly Father has in store for us—but we can be assured our quest will be worth the effort. He notes every tentative step we take and nudges and prods us in the direction of His favor. We, like the children in the game, are onto something wonderful, and He longs to see us claim what is rightfully ours.

"On your mark, get set, go!" A starting cap gun goes off, and the children scramble across the back lawn to find clues to the treasure awaiting them at the end of the map. They dart from tree to swing set to root cellar to stable to tree house to veranda until finally the treasure map cues them to head indoors.

Once inside the old house, the game is stepped up a notch—so many places to explore, so many clues to uncover. As they work their way upward, barely noticing they've now climbed two stories of the house, the kids can feel their hearts pumping adrenaline. Something truly wonderful must await them at the end of this adventure!

The final clues are the most difficult, and by now several players have dropped out from fatigue or being "eliminated." Just a few players have made it to the attic, where the real treasure lies.

"Wow!" they breathe as they push open the creaking door and see the cavernous space filled with odds and ends from generations gone by. But it takes persistence to comb through the cobwebs and dusty piles until finally they lay their hands on the prize.

Life is decidedly not a game. It's a serious matter, but the analogy works because we are indeed searching for treasure—the Bible calls it "the riches of his glory in Christ Jesus" (Philippians 4:19). Those riches include eternal life and so much more. Finding that prize is the foremost goal for the Christian. It takes a lot of effort, a lot of searching, and a lot of persistence to lay our hearts on it.

> *If you look for it as for silver and search for it as*
> *for hidden treasure, then you will understand the*
> *fear of the LORD and find the knowledge of God.*

> PROVERBS 2:4–5

"Dear Mother's are not the only arms I have flown to. But it does not seem as if God ought to take me in because I am in trouble, when I would not go to Him when I was happy in something else. But even in the midst of my greatest felicity I had many and many a misgiving, many a season when my conscience upbraided me for my willfulness toward my dear mother and my whole soul yearned for something higher and better even than Charley's love, precious as it was."

A conscience that alerts us when we step away from what is right is a gift we may not fully appreciate this side of heaven. Too often we see it as a nuisance instead—a schoolmarm in our heads that keeps us from saying or doing what we *really* want to say or do, one that won't allow us to get away with "white lies" or even slightly unethical conduct.

Why won't that nagging conscience shut up! Consider:

- The grocery store clerk gives back change for a twenty when we know we gave her a ten. Halfway to the car our inner schoolmarm speaks up: *Are you going to turn around and correct this or keep that money you know is not yours?*

- We lash out at a friend, saying more than we intended to—and using cruel words in the process. Her face shows how much our words stung. *Did I really just say what I think I said?*

- We neglect God when things are going our way but then run to Him with our laundry list once we get in a tight spot—begging Him to bless what we've already decided to do (whether it's His will or not). *Did God actually open this door, or am I bulldozing my way through it?*

A sensitive conscience, and the ability to heed it, is one of the greatest gifts God has given us. We do well to nurture this internal check and balance by keeping our spiritual ears attuned to its slightest nudge. The first time we ignore our conscience's warning bell, it may seem like a small thing. But if we continue the pattern, over time the voice of our conscience becomes harder and harder to hear. Isn't it so much better to *hear* our conscience. . .and then to heed it?

> *"I do my best always to have a clear conscience toward God and all people."*
>
> Acts 24:16 nrsv

20/20 Hindsight

"I have shut myself up in my room today to think over things. The end of it is that I am full of mortification and confusion of face. If I had only had confidence in Mother's judgment I should never have got entangled in this silly engagement. I see now that Charley never could have made me happy, and I know there is a good deal in my heart he never called out."

The choice of a mate is the most important decision we will make on this earth, after our decision to follow God. Finding our "missing rib" is nothing short of supernatural when we let God guide us to the right man or woman. And, as with all weighty decisions, we are wise if we seek the counsel of those with good judgment who know us best.

When God set our first two ancestors in the garden, He conducted the very first wedding and put His blessing on a union that remains a mystery even to this day—the "two become one flesh." We may even be shocked to discover that God's first commandment to the man and woman was to "be fruitful, and multiply" (Genesis 1:22 KJV). Translated, that means He commanded them to make love—and to keep making love—as they populated the earth and "took dominion" over it.

To God, the marital bond—and marital love—is a very serious thing.

As we all know, the story took an unexpected and unfortunate turn. The perfect union became very imperfect, and since that day relations between humans have been fraught with tension. Power struggles, selfishness, lies, and deceit—whatever ills can be heaped into the relational stew. And once there they only heat to a boil unless we allow the Master Chef to sweeten the ingredients, one day at a time.

Nobody sets out to have a bad marriage or a strained parent-child relationship or an insincere friendship. These things happen because real people—real *flawed* people like ourselves—are involved. And as long as we inhabit this earth, we will need the grace of God and the counsel of wise friends and loved ones to help keep us on the right track. Thankfully, both of these are available to us if we will but heed them.

Marriage should be honored by all,
and the marriage bed kept pure.

HEBREWS 13:4

Fly Away Home

*"After yesterday's passion of grief, shame, and anger,
I feel perfectly stupid and languid. Oh, that I was prepared
for a better world and could fly to it and be at rest!"*

How many times have we wished we could just "check out" of this harried life and fly straight to heaven—a one-way pass to the pearly gates? Sure, there are things we love about our earthly life, and in moments of mortal panic we cling to it, but it's such a struggle sometimes that we wonder. Even a first-century apostle struggled with this dilemma. "To go or to stay here," he wrote in a letter, "I'm torn over which is best—to stay here and help you grow closer to God, or to go on to heaven right now and *be* with God."

The twists and turns of our lives are not by mere chance, and even less so once we hitch our wagon to God's. He has promised to direct our steps and light our paths with His words, which means that even the hard times—those events and seasons we would rather forgo and certainly forget—were orchestrated by Him.

A hunter has a beloved dog. As the dog runs through the woods ahead of the hunter, he gets his paw caught in a bear trap. Following the sound of his dog's yelps, the hunter finds his trusty companion lying on the ground, his eyes begging for relief. When the hunter opens the trap, the dog thinks his misery is over—but for one horrible moment his master actually pushes his leg farther into the steel jaws in order to free the injured leg from the hinges. But the dog doesn't know that his temporary pain will be the path to his freedom.

We are the dog and the hunter is our heavenly Father. Will we trust that He knows what is best for us? Even in our pain, will we "cast our cares upon Him"—knowing that He cares for us? God sees the big picture and knows what wonders await us in the next life, but for now we are in training—a divine boot camp to test our mettle and build our character so that we, too, one day can "fly to [heaven] and be at rest."

Consider it pure joy, my brothers and sisters, whenever you face trials of many kinds, because you know that the testing of your faith produces perseverance.

JAMES 1:2–3

A Crisis of Belief

"Now that it is all over, how ashamed I am of the fury I have been in and which has given Amelia such advantage over me! I was beginning to believe that I was really living a feeble and fluttering but real Christian life and finding some satisfaction in it. But that is all over now. I am doomed to be a victim of my own unstable, passionate, wayward nature; and the sooner I settle down into that conviction, the better. And yet how my very soul craves the highest happiness and refuses to be comforted while that is wanting."

The surest mark of a "saving faith" is that our beliefs have passed through the crucible of doubt and testing—and come out tried and true. Until we go through our own dark night of the soul, the faith we lay claim to is not really ours; it is merely belief passed down to us from someone else's conviction.

A young woman faced a loss so devastating it shook her very foundations—everything she had been taught from childhood about God, all the verses and promises she had memorized, all her great expectations for how her life was supposed to be. And in the small, dark place she found herself in, there was little room left for hope. Her disappointments were too great. As she cast away her joy, along with it went her soul-deep assurance of God and how she fit into His big picture, if at all.

By happenstance, a friend loaned her a century-old book by a Scottish minister whose stories, it turned out, imparted greater spiritual truths than even his sermons. One character leaped off the page for her: a young man about her age who wrestled with his belief in God and whether he was truly born again.

In the midst of his struggle, a wise mentor encouraged him with words that rang in the young woman's heart, too: "Don't you realize that the very fact you are concerned with whether you are a Christian means that you most surely are?"

The old mentor's meaning was clear: if we didn't care about God—couldn't care less what He thought of us, much less if He even existed—our souls wouldn't be troubled enough to search out the truth. God sees our hearts, along with our "unstable, passionate, wayward nature," and He chooses us still—not to leave us as we are, but to mold us into the very image of His Son, Jesus Christ.

Let us hold unswervingly to the hope we profess,
for he who promised is faithful.

HEBREWS 10:23

Mad at God

*"'I am very glad to see you, my dear child,' [Dr. Cabot] said. I intended
to be very dignified and cold. As if I was going to have any of Dr.
Cabot's undertaking to sympathize with me! But those few kind words
just upset me, and I began to cry. 'You would not speak so kindly,'
I got out at last, 'if you knew what a dreadful creature I am. I am angry
with myself and angry with everybody and angry with God. I can't be
good two minutes at a time. I do everything I do not want to do and do
nothing I try and pray to do. Everybody plagues me and tempts me.
And God does not answer any of my prayers, and I am just desperate.'"*

Combing through the list of names mentioned in scripture's
"Heroes of the Faith" chapter is like reading a *Who's Who* of
tempestuous, strong-willed, cunning, criminal, washed-up,
lusty, *angry* sideliners—people we're sure would be picked last
for God's all-star team. And yet there they are, mentioned one
after another in a book that will stand the test of time, even
into eternity.

If the private record of history could be peeled back
and revealed, we'd probably be shocked to find that every
passionate believer was angry at God at some point in their
lives. Not just angry—that's too polite—but nail-spitting *mad*!

God is big enough to handle our anger, and He knows just

how to mold the lump of clay that is *us* on His potter's wheel. We may be in for a time of testing and stretching. We may cry and plead and bargain with God. We may even hear a "gird yourself like a man" speech out of the whirlwind, as Job did. But we can be sure that God takes us just as we are—warts and all—and will transform us into more than we ever thought we could be, for His kingdom, if we allow Him to.

The measure of our hearts as Christians isn't gauged on how we start the race, it's based on how we finish. And once we understand that, we begin to see how those tempestuous, strong-willed, cunning, criminal, washed-up, lusty, *angry* sideliners made it to the faith hall of fame. Perhaps when we make it to heaven and our own "books" are opened, we'll find out we did, too.

> *I have the desire to do what is good, but I cannot carry it out.*
> *For I do not do the good I want to do, but the evil I do*
> *not want to do—this I keep on doing.*

> Romans 7:18–19

The Everlasting Arms

"'Poor child!' he said in a low voice, as if to himself.
'Poor, heartsick, tired child that cannot see what I can see,
that its Father's loving arms are all about it!' I stopped crying
to strain my ears to listen. He went on. 'Katy, all that you say
may be true. I dare say it is. But God loves you. He loves you.'"

The God of the Old Testament is downright scary at times—a stern, righteous judge who seems bent on punishing those who step out of line. Yet the psalmist wrote love songs to Him and cherished his relationship with the Holy Spirit above everything else in his life. He likened himself to a sheep lovingly corralled and rescued, again and again, by the Lord, the Great Shepherd.

An Old Testament prophet watched as God, in His anger, caused the earth to open up and swallow thousands of people who disobeyed Him. Yet that same prophet begged God to allow him to see His face, he yearned for Him so much.

A king so rich and so wise he became legendary tried to find pleasure in "everything under the sun"—and concluded that only in God can true joy and satisfaction be found.

And then there's Jesus. Fierce and bold when He had to be, but known for being kind, meek, compassionate, and loving more than anything else.

Jesus told His followers, and us, that "anyone who has seen me has seen the Father" (John 14:9). That makes us consider that the same God who opened the earth in anger wept tears over a city forsaken because it rejected Him. And the same God who sits in judgment over sinners asked a woman caught in adultery, "Woman, where are your accusers?" When she answered, "There are none left" (they had all fled), He said, "Neither do I accuse you. Go and sin no more."

What good would it be to follow after a God who hurled lightning bolts but not love at His creation? In the person of Jesus we see the exact nature of God the Father: holy and righteous yet so full of *love* that our minds can't fathom it.

The same prophet who begged to see God's face lived to write these precious words: "The eternal God is your refuge, and underneath are the everlasting arms" (Deuteronomy 33:27). There's no safer place on earth or in heaven than in the everlasting arms of God.

The eternal God is your refuge,
and underneath are the everlasting arms.

DEUTERONOMY 33:27

The Prodigal's Purpose

"He loves me, I repeated to myself. He loves me. 'Oh, Dr. Cabot, if I could believe that! If I could believe that, after all the promises I have broken, all the foolish, wrong things I have done and shall always be doing, God perhaps still loves me!' 'You may be sure of it,' he said solemnly. 'I, His minister, bring the gospel to you today. Go home and say over and over to yourself, "I am a wayward, foolish child. But He loves me! I have disobeyed and grieved Him ten thousand times. But He loves me! I have lost faith in some of my dearest friends and am very desolate. But He loves me! I do not love Him; I am even angry with Him! But He loves me!"'"

The story of the prodigal son is one of the most poignant pictures Jesus gave us of God's true nature—and His love for us. Two sons growing up in their father's house had their every need provided for. Each son had an inheritance waiting for him when he came of age. One son, a steady hard worker, was content to stay close to home. But the other dreamed of greener pastures. When the restless son reached the age of full inheritance, he asked for his money and hit the road.

We all know the story—the younger brother squanders his inheritance on wild partying and women, and ends up feeding swine. We see God's true nature when the younger son returns home. As he approaches his house, the father sees him coming from afar and orders a great feast in his honor. The son begs his father for forgiveness and says he'll work as a slave on his father's estate, but the father reminds him that he is not a servant, not a part-time employee, but a *son*—and sonship always has privileges.

One of the more revealing details in this story is that when the father sees his son returning, he hikes up his robes and runs out to meet him. Overjoyed to see his wayward son, he doesn't scold or punish—he celebrates, forgives, restores.

When we go our own way, we carve a path of hardship for ourselves. But the moment we return to Him, choosing to walk in His ways, we feel the full favor of His blessings and grace and goodness upon us. Instead of scolding, the Father rushes out to meet us and love us back into His arms.

"Let's have a feast and celebrate. For this son of mine was dead and is alive again; he was lost and is found." So they began to celebrate.

Luke 15:23–24

A Full Heart

"I came away; and all the way home I fought this battle with myself, saying, 'He loves me!' I knelt down to pray, and all my wasted, childish, wicked life came and stared me in the face. I looked at it and said with tears of joy, 'But He loves me!' Never in my life did I feel so rested, so quieted, so sorrowful, and yet so satisfied."

The wisest man who ever lived said, "A word fitly spoken is like apples of gold in settings of silver" (Proverbs 25:11 NKJV). Truly, some words have the power to lift our spirits like nothing else. Some words will even change the course of our lives or revive a long-forgotten dream or hope. Other words simply make our day-to-day routines pleasant rather than burdensome.

A single mother oversleeps her alarm clock and struggles to get the kids off to school before showing up at work—late. She tries to slip past her supervisor unseen, but the man raises his head as she scurries past his office toward her cubicle.

The moment she boots up her computer, an e-mail from her supervisor pops into her in-box: *"Please come to my office as soon as you settle your things."* She wrings her hands. Worry sets in. This is the third time in recent months that she's been late. If she loses this job, she doesn't know what she'll do. How will she make ends meet beyond the next two weeks?

"You wanted to see me," she says from the doorway to his office, her head lowered.

"Yes, please come in and shut the door."

This is it, the woman thinks. *I'm about to be canned.*

The supervisor leans forward and laces his hands. In his eyes she sees compassion, not stern reprimand. *Could it be. . . ?*

"I'm starting a new flex-time schedule for all staff members, and I'd like you to set up your working hours. Some hours will be in-house, the others performed at home. As a single mother, I know. . ." The rest of his words grew faint and hazy in her mind as she felt her spirit lift and hope rekindle her heart. Everything was going to work out after all.

Each of us has the opportunity to be an agent of hope, encouragement, joy, and humor just by the words we speak. Let us choose our words carefully. Someone who crosses our path today may be in dire need of "a word fitly spoken."

A word fitly spoken is like apples
of gold in settings of silver.

PROVERBS 25:11 NKJV

Loving the Least of These

"What a beautiful world this is and how full it is of truly kind, good people. Mrs. Morris was here this morning, and just one squeeze of that long, yellow old hand of hers seemed to speak a book full! I wonder why I have always disliked her so, for she is really an excellent woman. I gave her a good kiss to pay her for the sympathy she had sense enough not to put into canting words; and if you will believe it, dear old Journal, the tears came into her eyes, and she said, 'You are one of the Lord's beloved ones, though perhaps you do not know it.'"

A young wife watched out her window as the old woman next door finally crept out of her house and puttered in the garden. Amid the tangled overgrowth, she appeared tiny and insignificant. A shut-in, the neighbors called her. Some even called her worse names, hinting that she had practiced the dark arts. Her tight white curls clung close to her head, and her eyes looked huge behind thick glasses.

Fueled by the wild neighborhood talk, the young wife imagined what went on behind the walls of her neighbor's house, relishing her sinister scenarios. She felt guilty for spying, but she couldn't tear herself away from the window. As the old woman made her way back into her house, she cast a backward glance over her shoulder in the direction of her spectator.

Caught! The young wife pulled away quickly, but she was not quick enough. The old woman had seen her, she knew, because for one brief moment their eyes had met. Fear fluttered in her heart. Two days later a folded note appeared at the young wife's front door. When she opened it, she read sweet words of greeting. *I'm so glad to have you for a neighbor,* it read. *Please come by for tea sometime.*

The very next day the young wife and the old woman shared stories over a pot of tea, and a friendship took shape— a friendship the young woman never forgot, for it taught her a lifelong lesson about loving those Jesus called "the least of these"—the shut-ins, the misfits, the forgotten.

We may not realize how much a simple smile or hug or handshake means to somebody else, so why not take the risk? We might find we've made a new friend!

Love does no wrong to a neighbor;
therefore, love is the fulfilling of the law.

ROMANS 13:10 NRSV

Beyond Understanding

"I repeated again to myself those sweet, mysterious words; and then I
tried to think what I could do for Him. But I could not think of anything
great or good enough. I went into Mother's room and put my arms round
her and told her how I loved her. She looked surprised and pleased.
'Ah, I knew it would come!' she said, laying her hand on her Bible.
'Knew what would come, Mother?' 'Peace,' she said."

In his letter to a group of new Christians, the apostle Paul
prayed a benediction over his readers, asking that the God
who empowered them would fill them with "peace that passes
all understanding." Paul endured unthinkable hardships—
starvation, beatings, shipwreck, wrongful incarceration, a
poisonous snakebite—and yet he floated along on a current of
calm and contentment and, above all, unbelievable peace.

What is this supernatural peace God bestows, and how
does it differ from the "peace" of the everyday world? We see
that the apostle's life was fraught with every danger imaginable,
yet it was also filled with supernatural interventions, miraculous
escapes, and angelic interactions. He walked and talked with
God as one who knew Him intimately, and his reward was an
unspeakable joy and incomprehensible peace.

God never promised we'd have an easy time as followers

in His name. In fact, He promised pretty much the opposite, warning that we would face opposition and persecution for believing in and following after His Son, Jesus, and going against the crowd. He assured us that "haters" would follow close at our heels the moment we took a stand for Him—but also that we should rejoice because our names are written in His eternal book.

God never promised us material wealth, but He assured us He would provide for our every need—even before we asked for it. He didn't promise us a fairy-tale ending either, but He guaranteed that those who choose Him will lead a life of meaning and purpose and destiny with eternal impact. And a life of unbelievable peace.

Paul died a martyr's death, yet if he had the chance for a do-over—a chance to live his life with a different "master" and an alternate outcome—no doubt he'd say, "I wouldn't change a thing." Could we say the same?

By prayer and petition, with thanksgiving, present your requests to God.
And the peace of God, which transcends all understanding,
will guard your hearts and your minds in Christ Jesus.

PHILIPPIANS 4:6–7

Propelled by Purpose

"I began to hem those handkerchiefs Mother asked me to finish a month ago. But I could not think of anything to do for God. I wish I could. It makes me happy to think, that all this time, while I was caring for nobody but myself and fancying He must almost hate me, He was loving and pitying me."

"Whatever your hand finds to do, do it with all your might," wrote Solomon, a man who learned the hard way that the only true joy in life comes from taking up our assigned work—our divine destiny's purpose—and seeing it through to the end.

There's something incredibly satisfying about starting, and finishing, a task well done. And when that job is undertaken "as to the Lord" (Colossians 3:23 KJV), it invigorates us body, soul, and spirit. Our earthly lives are a training ground, a boot camp, for something far greater. We catch little glimpses here and there of what God is preparing for us and that far-sighted perspective keeps the flame of our hope alive.

Make no mistake: this life is not all mountaintops and adventure. We will wade through many small streams—and even mud puddles—on the valley floor in between our hilltop escapades. But the mountain is there always, beckoning us to come up higher again.

For the moment we may be hemming handkerchiefs, or crunching numbers, or teaching reluctant children, or cleaning the garage—no matter. These mundane tasks add up to the sum of our lives, and as the years tick by, we hopefully see ourselves growing closer to God, hearing His voice more clearly, and stepping more fully into the real reason we are here.

If we look closely, we'll see that every time God used a man or woman to achieve great things in the Bible, they were already working when He approached them. "What is that in your hand?" (Exodus 4:2) He said to Moses—and called him to use the shepherd's staff for His purposes. When an angel appeared to Gideon, he was threshing wheat in secret. When a wealthy landowner saw the young widow Ruth from afar, she was gleaning in the fields. When Jesus called His first two disciples, they were throwing their fishing net into the sea.

"Work as if God were your employer," a good boss reminded a disgruntled employee one day. That simple word changed the employee's outlook and motivation. If we heed the same words, they will change our lives as well.

Whatever your hand finds to do,
do with your might.

ECCLESIASTES 9:10 NRSV

Mission Field Next Door

"'I only wanted to ask one thing,' I said. 'I want to do something for God. And I cannot think of anything unless it is to go on a mission. And Mother would never let me do that. She thinks girls with delicate health are not fit for such work.' 'At all events I would not go today,' he replied. 'Meanwhile do everything you do for Him who has loved you and given Himself for you.'"

The young man saw the poster the same day it appeared in the church's fellowship hall, and the images beckoned to him—hungry children with soulful eyes, eagerly waiting for food and a word about God. A group of teenagers, barefoot and wearing ragged clothing, but with smiles that lit up the dirt-poor village behind them. A mother with a huge bundle balanced on her head and a baby strapped to her back. He knew God was calling him to the mission field, and here was his opportunity at last.

We don't need to fly to China or Africa or New Guinea to "go to the mission field," even though some may be called to do just that. There's a mission field just outside our front doors, in our neighborhoods, at our workplaces, in our cities.

Before Jesus returned to His Father in heaven, He gave His disciples their marching orders, a passage that's come to be called the Great Commission. He told them to take the good news about His life, death, and resurrection to "Jerusalem, and in all Judea and Samaria, and to the ends of the earth" (Acts 1:8).

Moving outward in concentric circles, this ragtag band of former fishermen and tax collectors and day-laborers were commanded to start with where they were—the city they lived in—and gradually reach the outlying communities and remotest parts of the known world of their time. In that way the "mission of the commission" would be accomplished, one person at a time.

We don't need to pack our bags and leave town to impact the world for Christ. All it requires is seeing opportunities and seizing them—opportunities to tell someone about the God who loves them more than they can possibly imagine. When our daily routines become a "sermon without words," our whole lives are a mission field. Yes, we, too, are privileged to "do something for God."

Each of you should use whatever gift you have received to serve others, as faithful stewards of God's grace in its various forms.

1 PETER 4:10

The Good Life

"It has seemed to me for several days that it must be that I really do love God, though ever so little. But it shot through my mind today like a knife that it is a miserable, selfish love at the best, not worth my giving, not worth God's accepting."

The miracle of real love is that it overlooks flaws in others, seeing only the goodness in them and the joy they bring to our lives. That's the kind of love the toolmaker possessed. He met his future family as a widower in need of a reason to smile again, and he found it in their mother. Within eight months they were married, and he filled the spot labeled "dad" that had been vacated years earlier by their biological father.

The toolmaker was one of those rare people who just seemed to be "born good." Selfless almost to a fault, he had a smile and a kind word for everybody. If some chore or errand needed doing, he volunteered without waiting to see if someone else might do it. Children flocked to him—always a good sign of a person's character. And his eyes crinkled at the corners from a lifetime of laughter.

One day the toolmaker and his new wife attended a Sunday service at the church she belonged to, and for the first time in his life he really heard, and grasped, the message of the Gospel—how Jesus came to earth to die for the sins of all humankind. Oh, he'd been in church all his life, but somehow the takeaway was never anything more than "do good, be good, and say grace before meals." Now, suddenly, he was faced with the choice each of us is given: to say yes to Jesus and give Him first place in our lives, or to reject Him and live life on our terms. The toolmaker said yes. And his already kindhearted nature became lit from within by the presence of the One who gives life.

Each of us is given just one go at life. Like the adage says, life is not a dress rehearsal. We are here for only the briefest of moments on the timepiece of eternity, and how we live *today* matters—every single day. When our time comes, what will people say about us? For what will we be remembered?

> *Light dawns for the upright, for those who*
> *are gracious and compassionate and righteous.*
>
> PSALM 112:4

Wild Horses

*"'When I see a little infant caressing its mother, would you have me
to say to it, 'You selfish child, how dare you pretend to caress your mother
in that way? You are quite unable to appreciate her character; you love her
merely because she loves you, treats you kindly?' It was my turn to smile
now at my own folly. 'You are as yet but a babe in Christ,' Dr. Cabot
continued. 'You love your God and Savior because He first loved you.
The time will come when the character of your love will become changed
into one, which sees and feels the beauty and the perfection of its object;
and if you could be assured that He no longer looked on you with favor,
you would still cling to Him with devoted affection.'"*

Horse trainers know the best way to bring a wild horse
around is to lavish it with love, train it little by little with
kindness and boundaries—and then leave it alone and let
it come to you. The same principle works with people. In a
modern adaptation of *Sense & Sensibility*, the middle daughter,
Marianne, known for her tempestuous nature, is crushed to
learn that the man she'd set all her hopes on is a black-hearted
liar and cheat. Meanwhile, Colonel Brandon—who loves her
in secret—stands by and watches her cruel rejection and spiral
into depression. Finally, with no fight left in her, she welcomes
death. But with the care of her sister and the colonel, she

recovers at Colonel Brandon's manor house.

For weeks, they spend quiet afternoons together. His gentle nature and kind heart are a healing balm to her, and soon she grows content with the steady, patient, selfless love he extends.

On the day he returns her to her mother's care, Marianne turns to thank her friend. He nods curtly and departs—leaving her wondering what just happened. But the next time the two meet, it's obvious that she has fallen for her beloved friend, and yes, the story ends with a marriage (in fact, two).

Perhaps this is the way God deals with us. Indulgent while we are still spiritual babies, He gives us all the coddling and propping up we need. But once we mature into spiritual adulthood—when we know what our Lord requires of us—He pulls away ever so slightly to test our love for Him.

The LORD appeared to us in the past, saying: "I have loved you with an everlasting love; I have drawn you with unfailing kindness."

JEREMIAH 31:3

Beauty Inside and Out

"[Mother] says, too, that I am growing careless about my hair and my dress. But that is because my mind is so full of graver, more important things. I thought I ought to be wholly occupied with my duty to God. But Mother says duty to God includes duty to one's neighbor and that untidy hair, put up in all sorts of rough bunches, rumpled cuffs and collars, and all that sort of thing make one offensive to all one meets. I am sorry she thinks so, for I find it very convenient to twist up my hair almost any how, and it takes a good deal of time to look after collars and cuffs."

The average woman today will spend hundreds of dollars a year on beauty products and services, and for some that figure reaches into the thousands—all so she can be as physically attractive as possible. The beautiful faces and svelte bodies that peer from magazine pages and TV ads raise the bar ever higher.

Sadly, our modern culture promotes outer beauty at the expense of inner beauty. While waists get tinier and breasts get bigger, our self-esteem often grows thinner. Facing impossible standards and men trained to expect air-brushed female perfection, women look in the mirror and see every line, bulge, and dimple—not the beauty of the woman they are on the inside.

A teacher once told an allegory about how we are all born as tiny tree saplings—fresh, young, and green—and as we grow our trunk lengthens and our branches begin to spread out. Under ideal circumstances, we will one day resemble a mighty oak tree standing tall and strong. But the teacher saw something quite different as he gazed out at the world of people, all hurrying on their way. Instead of tall trees, most humans resembled twisted trunks, some nearly bent double by the years of care and worry and low self-esteem that stunted their growth like a parasite.

Only through the emotional healing provided by a loving heavenly Father could these twisted trunks be transformed, day by day, into the stately oaks they were intended to be. The same One who promised to "bind up the brokenhearted" (Isaiah 61:1) comes alongside, at our bidding, and applies a splint to straighten our twisted trunks. The One the psalmist said will restore our souls does just that. And over time we become the creation He made us to be, healthy and whole and beautiful—inside and out.

Charm is deceptive, and beauty is fleeting; but a
woman who fears the Lord is to be praised.

PROVERBS 31:30

Painful Progress

"Today I feel discouraged and disappointed. I certainly thought that if God really loved me and I really loved Him, I should find myself growing better day by day. But I am not improved in the least. Most of the time I spend on my knees I am either stupid, feeling nothing at all, or else my head is full of what I was doing before I began to pray or what I am going to do as soon as I get through. I do not believe anybody else in the world is like me in this respect."

The "Pilgrim's progress"—the lifelong walk of a Christian—is indeed fraught with twists and turns, pits and bogs, and only by steady plodding, and getting up when we fall down, will we make the finish line.

In his book by the same title, Puritan minister John Bunyan exhorts believers to stay the course even when distractions and setbacks come—and they most assuredly will. The protagonist, aptly named "Christian," sets out on his journey full of hope and faith. But along the way he must face a gauntlet of obstacles that could deter even the hardiest of souls. But God does not leave Christian helpless. The pilgrim receives supernatural help to keep his feet moving forward in the direction of heaven, which he ultimately attains.

Bunyan wrote his allegory with vivid imagery, so we are

right beside Christian, identifying with his every trial and of course his final victory. So often it feels as if our Christian journey is also one step forward, two steps back—even three steps back at times. We settle ourselves in to pray, and the minute we try to focus our minds on Jesus a swirl of minutiae converges on us. It's no coincidence that the moment we press in to God, our minds try to check out. In the spiritual realm, our unseen enemy conspires to trip us up, distract us, confuse us, tempt us, and hurt us every chance he gets. No other position scares him more than when he sees us on our knees.

But our Father in heaven is watching, too, and He sends "ministering angels" to help us when we need it most. Jesus Himself intercedes on our behalf, and the Holy Spirit fills us with His light and life. We are not left to our own devices, even though it sometimes feels that way. If God is for us, who can be against us?

If God is for us, who can be against us? He who did not spare his own Son, but gave him up for us all—how will he not also, along with him, graciously give us all things?

ROMANS 8:31–32

Baby Steps

"When I feel differently and can make a nice, glib prayer, with floods of tears running down my cheeks, I get all puffed up and think how much pleased God must be to see me so fervent in spirit. I go downstairs in this frame and begin to complain to our maid, Susan, for misplacing my music till all of a sudden I catch myself doing it and stop short, crestfallen and confounded. I have so many such experiences that I feel like a baby just learning to walk, who is so afraid of falling that it has half a mind to sit down once and for all."

When parents see their little ones taking those first halting steps, do they reprimand them because their gait is wobbly or they zig when they should zag and fall down with a plop? Of course not. Instead, parents predictably grin from ear to ear, whooping with joy, and capturing those precious first steps on their cameras.

So why do we often imagine God, our heavenly Father, as a stern, even cruel, parent instead of a loving one? Can we not see that we are made in His image?

As Jesus talked to a group of followers one day, He made this very point because they, too, imagined God as remote, harsh, and exacting—demanding perfection while we struggle to take even baby steps.

Jesus asked the people, "Which of you, if your son asks for bread, will give him a stone?" (Matthew 7:9). He made it real to them, framing the question in a scenario they could understand—a father and son in a simple everyday setting.

He continued: "Which of you fathers, if your son asks for a fish, will give him a snake instead?" (Luke 11:11). The very thought was shocking, so far from any normal parent's response that it was preposterous.

And suddenly we see it. Like the people sitting around Jesus that day, in their "aha" moment of truth, we realize that God is a parent, too, and that our every halting step in the direction of Christlikeness is a reason to shout and whoop with joy—a reason to beam with pride, a reason to capture our progress on a celestial videotape and record it in our heavenly book.

The eyes of the LORD are on those who fear him,
on those whose hope is in his unfailing love.

PSALM 33:18

Goodness versus Happiness?

"I want to please God and to be like Him. I certainly do. But I am so young, and it is so natural to want to have a good time! And now I am in for it, I may as well tell the whole story. When I read the lives of good men and women who have died and gone to heaven, I find they all like to sit and think about God and about Christ. Now I don't. I often try, but my mind flies off in a tangent. The truth is I am perfectly discouraged."

The young woman felt God tugging at her heart, calling her back to the childlike faith that once burned bright and full in her life. She remembered the simple prayers she prayed at her bedside—sometimes with her mother, sometimes alone with God—and how sweet those times were. But that was before everything got all messed up; life got complicated then turned ugly. The fairy tales she'd believed as a little girl turned out to be lies; or perhaps they were reserved for someone else, not her. Why should she believe God would turn out to be "good" either?

Yet the pull of the Holy Spirit was too strong. Feeling His gentle tug, she drove to a nearby sanctuary that held weeknight rallies for college-aged men and women. As she steered into a parking space, one thought crossed her mind: *I bet all the guys will be homely. There's no way CHRISTIAN guys can be cool or good-looking.*

Slinging her purse over her shoulder, she walked toward

the building and heard the throb of music from a band playing inside. *Hmm, interesting.*

She pushed through the main door, and as she rounded a corner she nearly plowed into a tall, handsome young man—the handsomest guy she'd ever seen. Her breath caught in her throat.

Over the ensuing months, a sweet love story played out between her and the handsome young man, who was unlike any man she'd ever known. Was it possible that God could send someone both good *and* good-looking across her path? She'd always believed, in a twisted way, that it had to be one or the other—bad and cute, or good and homely.

We struggle to believe that God loves us so much He delights to bring us good gifts so amazing they leave us breathless. We stand in awe when He showers us, or those we love, with blessings so abundant they cannot be contained.

Oh, taste and see that the LORD is good;
blessed is the man who trusts in Him!

PSALM 34:8 NKJV

Quiet Heroism

" 'You must make the most of what little Christian life you have; be thankful God has given you so much, cherish it, pray over it, and guard it like the apple of your eye. Imperceptibly, but surely it will grow and keep on growing, for this is its nature,' [Mrs. Cabot said]. 'But I don't want to wait,' I said despondently. 'I have just been reading a delightful book, full of stories of heroic deeds—not fables, but histories of real events and real people. It has quite stirred me up and made me wish to possess such beautiful heroism that I might have a chance to perform some truly noble, self-sacrificing acts.' 'I dare say your chance will come,' she replied."

Without the use of time-lapse photography, it requires a lot of patience to watch a seed grow into a plant. We push the seed into a bed of dark rich soil, water it, and make sure it gets the proper sunshine. For days we see nothing, but the seed is not dead—or idle. Beneath the soil, something wonderful is happening: life is stirring.

Suddenly one day we see a tiny green shoot, just the smallest of sprouts. It doesn't look like much, but it's a start. We check for growth every day, but it appears the same. Then one magical day we realize the shoot has changed; it's now half an inch in height whereas before it barely broke the surface of the soil. Within a few years the plant or tree will be fully grown, bearing fruit or flowers or shade, and perhaps even providing an ecosystem for other smaller life forms. It accomplished something quietly heroic, simply by allowing God to bring forth its intended purpose.

God works the same way in us. We wonder how God can take us from our clumsy spiritual beginnings and help us grow "mature, attaining to the whole measure of the fullness of Christ" (Ephesians 4:13). Yet the same God who makes that promise also said He would complete the spiritual work begun in us. In other words, He will take that seed of faith and allow it to break open in our hearts and send up tiny green shoots.

Over the years, if we remain under the care of our Gardener, we will grow mature and bear fruit. While we were busy with life—slipping and falling but always getting up—God Himself pulled off a quiet heroism by fulfilling His purpose in and through us.

Good people will grow like palm trees. . . . Like trees planted in the Temple of the LORD, they will grow strong in the courtyards of our God. When they are old, they will still produce fruit.

PSALM 92:12–14 NCV

Homely Things

⤳⤳⤳

*"'Suppose, then, you content yourself for the present with doing in a
faithful, quiet, persistent way all the little, homely tasks that return with
each returning day, each one as unto God, and perhaps by and by you will
thus have gained strength for a more heroic life,' [said Mrs. Cabot]."*

Oswald Chambers, a turn-of-the-century Scottish minister,
turned his attention to the mundane, simple things of life again
and again. Thriving in the mundane is a constant theme in his
writings, and we can only imagine that theme came from the
reality of living out this "school of hard knocks" lesson in his
day-to-day life.

"Sometimes we are fresh and eager to attend a prayer
meeting, but do we feel that same freshness for such mundane
tasks as polishing shoes?" Chambers writes. "Being born again
from above is an enduring, perpetual, and eternal beginning.
It provides a freshness all the time in thinking, talking, and
living—a continual surprise of the life of God. Staleness is an
indication that something in our lives is out of step with God."

In our high-blown culture of instant celebrity and get-rich-
quick schemes, there's a very real tendency for us as believers
to expect the same—all for God's glory, of course. We forget
that His divine purpose may involve "littleness" here on earth

but greatness in the kingdom of heaven. Yes, we have to remember that this earthly sojourn is not the end of the line. In fact, it's just the beginning.

Jesus raised the dead and healed the sick, drawing huge crowds of eager followers, but He also took up a towel and washed dirty feet. His obedience in the little things, even something as inglorious as serving others, made it possible for Him to accomplish the big things when the time came.

Chambers writes: "We all have those times when there are no flashes of light and no apparent thrill to life, where we experience nothing but the daily routine with its common everyday tasks." He's right. We shouldn't expect God to give us all thrilling moments. Instead we must learn to live in the common times by His power. It's often in those random circumstances of life, when we are not distracted by lofty pursuits and our lives are quiet, that we have time to really appreciate the work of God in our lives.

> *"Be still, and know that I am God! I am exalted*
> *among the nations, I am exalted in the earth."*
>
> PSALM 46:10 NRSV

A Life Well Lived

" 'Then, dear Katy, suppose your first act of heroism tomorrow should be gratifying your mother in these little things, little though they are. Surely your first duty, next to pleasing God, is to please your mother and in every possible way to sweeten and beautify her life. You may depend upon it that a life of real heroism and self-sacrifice must begin and lay its foundation in this little world wherein it learns its first lesson and takes its first steps,' [said Mrs. Cabot]."

In the 1950s, five young men flew to a remote jungle in Ecuador to evangelize the Huaorani people, an indigenous group considered to be savage and violent to outsiders. After overtures of their peaceful intent met with friendly responses from the Huaorani, the men prepared to live close to the people and gradually teach them the Gospel of Jesus Christ. The men believed their years of preparation and zeal for the Lord were about to pay off. Their journal entries capture their dedication and excitement for the task at hand—which promised also to be the adventure of a lifetime.

Jim Elliot, who became the most famous of the five men, wrote on October 28, 1949: "He is no fool who gives what he cannot keep to gain that which he cannot lose." His words would be put to the test. On January 8, 1956, after a promising start, Elliot and his four companions were killed by a group of Huaorani warriors. Their bodies were found lying in a stream.

By outward appearance, their grand missionary adventure was a total failure. But the story doesn't end there. After her husband's death, Elisabeth Elliot spent two years as a missionary to the tribe members who killed her husband. Her steadfast love in the face of such a horrific act won over the hearts of the people, and along with other missionaries she was able to see many of the Huaorani people become followers of Christ. Jim Elliot's own spiritual legacy lives on, and his martyr death has had far-reaching effects.

Oftentimes what we see as failure is a stepping-stone to something much greater in God's eternal playbook. Unlike us, He sees the big picture and knows the end from the beginning. He plants each of His children in exactly the right spot at exactly the right time to accomplish His purposes for "such a time as this."

We know that in all things God works for the good of those who love him, who have been called according to his purpose.

ROMANS 8:28

Feeble Petitions

"[Mrs. Cabot replied,] 'My dear child, what a question! If there is any one truth I would gladly impress on the mind of a young Christian, it is just this, that God notices the most trivial act, accepts the poorest, most threadbare little service, listens to the coldest, feeblest petition, and gathers up with parental fondness all our fragmentary desires and attempts at good works. Oh, if we could only begin to conceive how He loves us, what different creatures we should be!'"

God's loving care is played out day after day, night after night, in the quiet hours—and the busy hours—when we're not (always) watching ourselves. God sends helpers to do His bidding in the most unexpected ways.

A man strides across his yard to clean his grill for an upcoming barbecue. By chance, as he passes under a large oak tree, he glances down and suddenly pulls back his foot before it strikes the ground. There, lying in the grass, still wet from birth, are two tiny baby cardinals that have fallen from their nest. Looking up, the man hears the mother cardinal's loud chirping and now understands that what he took for the sounds of nature was actually a distress call. He brings a tall ladder, scoops the babies into his hand, and lovingly places them back in their nest high in the oak tree.

The story of the rescued baby birds reached the man's neighbor, and a week later she asked him what became of the little birds. Did they make it? Or did the mother bird perhaps push them out of the nest—again?

"No, no, they were fine," said the man. "In fact, a few days later I saw them hopping around the yard, and then they flew off. The mother taught 'em how to fly fast!"

Not every story has a happy ending, and not every "feeble petition" we cast heavenward will be answered according to our preferences, but we can know this: God sees and hears everything—even the unspoken prayers of our hearts. He will answer in His perfect timing, in His perfect way. Those things that don't make sense to our human minds, we have to leave in His hands and trust that God knows what He's doing. And for those burdens that seem too heavy to bear, we have the privilege of dropping them at His feet.

The eyes of all look to you, and you give them their food in due season.
You open your hand, satisfying the desire of every living thing.

PSALM 145:15–16 NRSV

The Short List

"Mother is very much astonished to see how nicely I am keeping things in order. I was flying about this morning, singing and dusting the furniture, when she came in and began, 'He that is faithful in that which is least'—but I ran at her with my brush and would not let her finish. I really, really don't deserve to be praised. For I have been thinking that, if it is true that God notices every little thing we do to please Him, He must also notice every cross word we speak, every shrug of the shoulders, every ungracious look, and that they displease Him. And my list of such offenses is as long as my life!"

If God is keeping a long account of our every failing, we're all in trouble! But, happily for us, that is not the case. As we dig into the words of God we find that just the opposite is true— when we call ourselves by His name.

Thank goodness for the sea of forgetfulness. If we align ourselves with the Lord and follow His ways, asking His forgiveness for our sins, He promises to remove those sins from us and throw them into this mysterious sea described in the Bible (see Micah 7:19). God says our sins are removed "as far as the east is from the west" (Psalm 103:12)—in other words, irretrievably. And that goes for all our sins, the heavy-duty stuff as well as the garden-variety offenses.

One of the easiest comparisons we can use to understand God's heart toward us is that of a mom or dad with an infant. Babies are completely dependent on their parents. If the child cries, the parents don't punish her; they pick her up, pat her bottom, and comfort her. They feed her when she's hungry, change her diaper when it's dirty, and swaddle her in a warm blanket when she's cold.

As the child learns to walk, no loving parent would punish her for falling down now and then. Instead they grab the video camera and shout for joy: their baby took her first step! Soon the toddler can run and climb and form sentences. She will pout and whine now and then, but she's still their precious child.

Our God is a forbearing God, full of love and provision and correction, when needed, but even His correction is so loving it will cause us to rejoice—if not now, then at some future point in our lives.

> *"You are a forgiving God, gracious and compassionate,*
> *slow to anger and abounding in love."*
>
> NEHEMIAH 9:17

The Divine Paradox

"Mother has been very patient and forbearing with me all day. Tonight, after tea, she said in her gentlest, tenderest way, 'Dear Katy, I feel very sorry for you. But I see one path which you have not yet tried, which can lead you out of these sore straits. You have tried living for yourself a good many years, and the result is great weariness and heaviness of soul. Try now to live for others. Take a class in the Sunday school. Go with me to visit my poor people. You will be astonished to find how much suffering and sickness there is in the world and how delightful it is to sympathize with and try to relieve it.'"

Jesus made it clear to His followers that those who long to be first shall be last, and those who are last shall be first; those who are poor in spirit will gain the riches of heaven; those who lose their lives for His sake shall find them; and those who give are more blessed than those who receive.

When He created us, God designed us with an innate need to look outward (to other people) and upward (to Him)—not at our own navel. Yet that very tendency wields a powerful influence in our lives. What's the best cure for self-centeredness? Purposeful other-centeredness!

A woman found herself bored and wanting to be useful. "Why not help with our girls' group," a friend at church suggested. The woman doubted her ability to relate to a group of first- and second-grade girls, but with her friend's encouragement she took the plunge. The program was aimed at teaching young girls how to live godly lives while doing crafts and singing songs and working through a simple curriculum. But the best part of the class was the girls themselves. Generous with their smiles, honest with their feelings, the girls drew her into their lives in a way she'd never known before.

One day the shyest girl in the class pulled her aside and shared a painful situation in her home life. That single moment of intimacy between teacher and student bonded the two, and the teacher knew she had been given a rare gift: a child's trust.

By the end of the first year, the woman realized she'd never been happier than when she was teaching "her girls," as she came to think them. She forgot what her life had been like all those months ago when she was bored.

Let each of you look not to your own interests,
but to the interests of others.

PHILIPPIANS 2:4 NRSV

Childlike Hearts

"I have taken it at last. I would not take one before, because I knew I could not teach little children how to love God unless I loved Him myself. My class is perfectly delightful. There are twelve dear little things in it of all ages between eight and nine. Eleven are girls, and the one boy makes me more trouble than all of them put together. When I get them all about me and their sweet innocent faces look up into mine, I am so happy that I can hardly help stopping every now and then to kiss them. They ask the very strangest questions! I mean to spend a great deal of time in preparing the lesson and in hunting up stories to illustrate it. Oh, I am so glad I was ever born into this beautiful world, where there will always be dear little children to love!"

For years Hollywood movies depicted Jesus as a long-faced, somber-eyed man who seemed more depressing to be around than uplifting. And, more importantly, that portrayal of Jesus doesn't line up with what scripture tells us about this man who was both God and human—namely that *children were drawn to Him.* Enter the Jesus films of the 1990s and new millennium. Now for the first time, we see Jesus laughing, crying, joshing with His disciples, and beaming with delight when little children ran to Him to sit on His lap and listen to His stories.

Movies aside—if the Son of God were to walk in our midst today, as He did in the first century, wouldn't we expect Him to be someone who commanded our respect and awe even as He washed our feet and dined with alcoholics? A man who wasn't afraid to mingle with the homeless as well as millionaires? A man who children felt comfortable being around?

Jesus Himself raised the bar for true spirituality when He said that anyone who wants to enter the kingdom of heaven must "become like little children" (Matthew 18:3). As He spoke, no doubt He held a little one on His lap while teaching the crowd gathered on the hillside.

If we have ears to hear, His point is not lost on us today: we come to Christ the same way a child approaches a new friend—heart wide open, full of expectation, and ready to trust.

> *Jesus said, "Let the little children come to Me, and do not forbid them; for of such is the kingdom of heaven."*
>
> MATTHEW 19:14 NKJV

Growing Better, Not Older

"Now that I have these twelve little ones to instruct, I am more than ever in earnest about setting them a good example through the week. It is true they do not, most of them, know how I spend my time nor how I act. But I know; and whenever I am conscious of not practicing what I preach, I am bitterly ashamed and grieved. How much work, badly done, I am now having to undo! If I had begun in earnest to serve God when I was as young as these children are, how many wrong habits I should have avoided, habits that entangle me now as in so many nets. I am trying to take each of these little gentle girls by the hand and to lead her to Christ. Poor Johnny Ross is not so docile as they are and tries my patience to the last degree."

Each of us has a faith-walk timeline—with some trusting in Jesus for so long it predates their earliest memories. Others can recount dramatic "Damascus Road" conversions that leave listeners hanging on their every word. And some are still contemplating the decision.

Regardless of when we say yes to Jesus, once we do we enter the spiritual school of hard knocks. We'll find blessings and favor and goodness along the way, but hardship and suffering, too. And sometimes, it seems, the hardest test of all is battling our own sin-bound human nature as we reach upward toward Christlikeness.

Theologian and professor Howard G. Hendricks said, "Perhaps the Spirit of God is saying to many of us today, 'I want to minister through you. But before I can minister through you, I must minister to you.' Don't despise the educational experience of your drying brook. Don't throw in the towel. . . . He wants to make you just like His Son."

The apostle Paul wrote of "joy unspeakable and full of glory" (1 Peter 1:8 KJV), the promised blessing for every believer whose faith is tested by fire, being more precious than gold, and resulting in the salvation of our souls. Why the joy? Because every day we're growing more and more into the likeness of our Lord.

The choice is ours: live life our own way, indulging our pleasures and paying the consequences, or enroll in God's curriculum and fulfill His purpose for our lives, hearing the words "well done, good and faithful servant" when we stand before Him.

Let perseverance finish its work so that you may
be mature and complete, not lacking anything.

JAMES 1:4

Accepted in the Beloved

"This has been a delightful Sunday. I have really feasted on Dr. Cabot's preaching. But I am satisfied that there is something in religion I do not yet apprehend. I do wish I positively knew that God had forgiven and accepted me."

Why is it we struggle to forgive ourselves once God has said, "I forgive you"? Perhaps because guilt is so deeply imbedded in our human nature we can't imagine He really means it—and even if He does, well, we certainly remember our transgression!

Forgiving ourselves begins with grasping on a heart-deep level that God has truly forgiven us. All the times we lied or cheated, all the times we hurt someone with our words or actions, every vile or ungracious thought—if we start to tally our wrongs, we may get so depressed we never crawl out of the pity hole. Yet God makes it so simple. He says that if we confess our sins, He is faithful and just to forgive them. . . because Christ already paid the penalty for our sin debt.

But has He *really* forgiven us? we wonder. Could it possibly be that simple? If God won't punish us, perhaps we'd better do so ourselves, as the monks did with their misguided self-flagellation.

Imagine what life must have been like for the newly

converted Saul of Tarsus. When we read his later epistles—
the letters that make up so much of the New Testament—we
realize that many years had passed and Saul (now called Paul)
had matured spiritually. But in those early days, when the other
believers were frightened of him, afraid to trust him, we can
imagine how he suffered in silence. The burden of guilt from
his past as a murderer of Christians must have been a weighty
albatross around his neck.

Yet somewhere along the way Paul "got it"—he caught the
truth of what Christ had done for him, and for all of us, on the
cross. And that changed everything. Because of that revelation
he was able to pen words of blazing hope and righteousness:
namely that all who believe on the Lord Jesus Christ are not
condemned but are rather "accepted in the beloved." Accepted
by God; accepted in the "household of faith" among other
believers; accepted, at last, by ourselves.

To the praise of the glory of his grace,
wherein he hath made us accepted in the beloved.

Ephesians 1:6 KJV

Pressing On

"People talk about happiness to be found in a Christian life. I wonder why I do not find more! On Sundays I am pretty good and always seem to start afresh; but on weekdays I am drawn along with those about me. All my pleasures are innocent ones; there is surely no harm in going to concerts, driving out, singing, and making little visits! But these things distract me; they absorb me; they make religious duties irksome. I almost wish I could shut myself up in a cell and so get out of the reach of temptation. The truth is, the journey heavenward is all uphill. I have to force myself to keep on. The wonder is that anybody gets there with so much to oppose—so little to help one!"

Left to our own devices, we would take the fast route, the broad way that leads to destruction, because every molecule of our humanity prefers ease to resistance and leisure to hard work. But God loves us too much to leave us to our own devices.

Beyond the honeymoon phase of our Christian walk, where everything seems sweet and light, we encounter the reality of growing up in God. He brings out the hammer, the file, and turns up the heat in the crucible. There, in the furnace of His love and correction, we are purified and made ready for His use.

But, you might ask, with the journey toward godliness "all uphill," how does anyone actually make it? With all the temptation and distraction and busyness of this earthly life, how do any of us reach the hilltop?

The answer is that by ourselves we can't. And we don't—unless we have a divine Helper who comes alongside us, takes us by the hands, and gently pulls us up the mountain. Step by wavering step, sometimes tripping over rocks and falling into potholes, we are tugged up the mountain until we are conformed to the image of Christ.

A young bride receives the horrible news that her husband, a missionary, has been murdered by the tribal people he went to evangelize. Yet years later, this same woman wrote that even in suffering, there is a sense in which everything is a gift.

What will our confession be when the storm comes? Will we find ourselves steady and strong because we "built our house on the Rock," or will everything we use to prop up our identity as Christians be swept away by the tide?

"The rain came down, the streams rose, and the winds blew and beat against that house; yet it did not fall, because it had its foundation on the rock."

MATTHEW 7:25

Coming to the Crossroads

"It is high time to stop and think. I have been like one running a race and am stopping to take breath. I do not like the way in which things have been going on of late. I feel restless and ill at ease. I see that if I would be happy in God, I must give Him all. And there is a wicked reluctance to do that. I want Him—but I want to have my own way, too. I want to walk humbly and softly before Him, and I want to go where I shall be admired and applauded. To whom shall I yield? To God? Or to myself?"

Tucked away in the words of Luke's Gospel, we find these troubling words: "To whom much is given, from him much will be required" (Luke 12:48 NKJV). As believers, we may go along for years in a kind of status-quo existence, doing the "Christian" thing and feeling pretty good about ourselves. But the day comes when we arrive at a fork in the road: do we go left and pursue the good life of our own making, accumulating things and living for ourselves, or do we turn right down the straight, narrow, stony path of God's will—no matter what that may be?

God Himself brings us to this fork in the road. All along He's been honing us, molding us, pruning us to make us more like His Son, Jesus. The farther we travel down His path, the more we see old habits and bad character traits drop off us like discarded clothing. He is gracious enough to help us, and often we don't even realize the transformation until someone remarks about how much we've changed.

And then—the fork in the road. We've come so far, and God has brought us to this point. Now He wants to see which way we will choose on our own. Babes in the woods no more, we're fully "grown-up" believers and have to make grown-up decisions about what we allow to lodge in our minds, how to react when provoked, what we do when God allows hardship to fall upon us.

Jesus' disciples came to such a fork in the road on the night He was crucified. For three years, they had chosen to follow Him. But would they acknowledge Him now to the angry crowd? Were they willing to follow Him to the cross? Judas went down the wrong path. Peter, too—though briefly. Now it's our turn to make that tough choice.

This is what the LORD says: "Stand at the crossroads and look;
ask for the ancient paths, ask where the good way is,
and walk in it, and you will find rest for your souls."

JEREMIAH 6:16

Little Prayers

"[Dr. Cabot said,] 'No, child, go on singing; God has given you this power of entertaining and gratifying your friends. But pray without ceasing that you may sing from pure benevolence and not from pure self-love.' 'Why, do people pray about such things as that?' I cried. 'Of course they do. Why, I would pray about my little finger if my little finger went astray.' I looked at his little finger but saw no signs of its becoming schismatic."

When we look back over our lives as believers, our minds flit to the big highs and standout lows, but what about the little moments? Do we recall those sweet and sublime "small moments" when God answered a little prayer in a big way?

An adolescent girl felt her newfound faith in God stretched one day when she realized she'd lost her new gym suit at school. After gym, she'd stuffed it in a plastic bag to take home and wash, but in the rush between classes the striped knit gym suit got lost.

The girl panicked. Her mom had scraped together the money for the new gym suit so she wouldn't have to wear the ugly hand-me-down suit from her older sister—a move that would have made her the laughingstock of the seventh grade with its outdated style and faded colors. She had been so proud to parade around the athletic field in her bright blue striped gym suit, matching all the other girls, and now here she'd gone and lost it in the first two weeks of school.

A thought pricked her conscience. *I could pray about it.* But she quickly dismissed it. God couldn't possibly be interested in such a little thing as a gym suit. *"Ask Me,"* she heard a still, small voice whisper in her spirit. And so she prayed, asking God to help her find the gym suit.

Two days passed with no answer in sight, and then on Thursday, as she sat in English class, she suddenly remembered: *I stuffed it in my Social Studies desk!*

When the bell rang, the girl ran down the hall to her Social Studies class and peered into the bottom of her desk. There, stuffed into a far corner, was the plastic bag holding her gym suit.

Clutching the clothing to her chest, she smiled. *God really does answer prayer.* Big or little, significant or mundane, our petitions matter to Him.

> *When you call upon me and come*
> *and pray to me, I will hear you.*
>
> JEREMIAH 29:12 NRSV

The Christmas Visit

"Today I am twenty. That sounds very old, yet I feel pretty much as I did before. I have begun to visit some of Mother's poor folks with her and am astonished to see how they love her and how plainly they let her talk to them. As a general rule I do not think poor people are very interesting, and they are always ungrateful. . . . But on the whole I am glad I went with Mother because it has gratified her. Besides, one must either stop reading the Bible altogether or else leave off spending one's whole time in just doing easy, pleasant things one likes to do."

The single adults' Bible study faced a choice about how they would spend Christmas Eve—hosting a festive bonfire with feasting and games and midnight carols around the fire, or visiting a nursing home. Put to a vote, the bonfire won by a landslide, but as the calendar closed in on December 24th, the group knew what they should do—bring a little Christmas cheer to a roomful of forgotten elderly people.

They arrived at the nursing home in late afternoon, toting finger foods and song sheets for the caroling. But somehow signals had gotten crossed, and no one at the nursing home was expecting them—nor had they prepared the residents.

"Well, can we stay and visit anyway?" the leader of the singles' group asked. "Why waste all this good food?"

The woman behind the desk hesitated. "I'm not sure. . . . Many of the residents retire to their rooms early, but I'll send a message over the PA and see who comes."

The superintendent's voice sounded over the PA system: "A group of young people from a local church are in the rec room, and they have food and Christmas songs to share with you. Anyone interested?"

Within minutes, wheelchair after wheelchair rolled into the room, and those residents who could walk made their way with the help of walkers or canes. The singles put a song sheet and plate of finger foods into every resident's hand, smiling as they introduced themselves. A young man with a guitar starting playing, and a woman sat at the piano to accompany him. The residents sat silent at first but grew bolder with each song.

That Christmas, the single adults had no bonfire, but they left the nursing home with warmth in their hearts. Sometimes we think we are blessing others when really we are the ones who are blessed beyond measure.

A generous person will prosper; whoever refreshes others will be refreshed.

PROVERBS 11:25

The Critical Hour

"[Susan Green replied,] 'I'm a-dying? Why, it beats all my calculations. I was going to live ever so many years and save up ever so much money, and then, when my time came, I was going to put on my best fluted nightgown and nightcap and lay my head on my handsome pillow and draw the clothes up over me, neat and tidy, and die decent. But here's my bed all in a toss, and my frills all in a crumple, and my room all upside down, and bottles of medicine setting around alongside of my vases, and nobody here but you, just a girl, and nothing else!' All this came out by jerks, as it were, and at intervals. 'Don't talk so!' I fairly screamed. 'Pray, pray to God to have mercy on you!'"

Death creeps in and catches us unawares at times—the loss of a friend or acquaintance or loved one—and we reel from its finality. Other times we see it on the horizon well in advance and prepare for it, or so we think. But when it comes, we are reminded anew of how frail our mortality is and that life—this earthly life we cherish and cling to—is but a breath away from eternity.

What we say to those who are searching for the truth— or rather, Truth—matters every moment we spend in their company, but there comes a time when death waits just beyond the door. We have entered "the critical hour," those minutes or even seconds before the person's life here on earth is extinguished and they are ushered into eternity. What will we say to them in those moments? What a privilege it is to be able to speak the name of Jesus and "pray, pray to God to have mercy" on our friend or loved one.

At times, what King Solomon called the "fear of man" (Proverbs 29:25) keeps our mouths shut tight when we might instead tell our friends about Jesus. That is just the right time to start praying, first for ourselves that we will be emboldened to speak those precious words that have the power to open the gates of heaven for someone. Once we have prayed for ourselves and spoken those words, it's time to pray that God would prepare the soil of that heart to receive them.

> *We saw it, we heard it, and now we're telling you so*
> *you can experience it along with us, this experience of*
> *communion with the Father and his Son, Jesus Christ.*
>
> 1 JOHN 1:3 MSG

A Father's Passing

"Mother met me with open arms when I reached home. She was much shocked at what I had to tell and at my having encountered such a scene alone. I should have felt myself quite a heroine under her caresses if I had not been overcome with bitter regret that I had not, with firmness and dignity, turned poor Susan's last thoughts to her Savior. Oh, how could I, through miserable cowardice, let those precious moments slip by!"

The last day she saw him, a daughter couldn't help but notice the dazed look on her father's face. He had mowed the lawn in the blazing heat of a Florida summer and then sank into his favorite armchair, his eyes holding a strange, faraway look. The next morning: a phone call. Dad was gone, her mom told her, having slipped away in his sleep with a half smile still on his face. A stroke took his earthly life, but it couldn't rob his legacy. A simple man, that smile spoke volumes about the life he had lived—the life of one who gave more than he took and spread goodness in his wake.

Numb from the news, the daughter threw herself into her work. Tears wouldn't come, and didn't come, until the day of her father's memorial service. Finally, surrounded by friends and family, she sobbed tears of sadness and tears of joy, for she knew he was in the presence of his Lord at last.

Renowned pastor and author Erwin Lutzer said that our idea that Jesus will greet us on the other side is misleading. After all, He walks with us here on this side of the curtain. And when the time comes, He guides us through. What a wonderful insight. And what a wonderful reason to introduce our dying friends and loved ones to Him. Why should they face the end of their lives alone when they could have the presence of God there with them, reassuring them, comforting them, and softly leading them into the presence of God, our heavenly Father?

The legacy we leave here on earth is important. Each day is a fresh opportunity to sow seeds of kindness into the lives of those we leave behind. But we can also acquire a heavenly legacy by speaking words of life to those whose lives are coming to an end.

Yea, though I walk through the valley of the shadow of death, I will fear no evil; for You are with me; Your rod and Your staff, they comfort me.

PSALM 23:4 NKJV

The Twinkling of an Eye

"I have learned one thing, by yesterday's experience, that is worth knowing. It is this: Duty looks more repelling at a distance than when fairly faced and met. Of course I have read the lines, 'Nor know we anything so fair as is the smile upon thy face'; but I seem to be one of the stupid sort who never apprehend a thing till they experience it. Now, however, I have seen the smile and find it so 'fair' that I shall gladly plod through many a hardship and trial to meet it again. Poor Susan! Perhaps God heard my eager prayer for her soul and revealed Himself to her at the very last moment."

At a church potluck, a group of women talked among themselves and caught up on all the news. "Poor Mr. Smith," said one, sighing. "He died Saturday night. The man never had time for God, but he sure found out the truth when he crossed over, didn't he?"

"Stop!" said another woman in the group. "We don't know where Mr. Smith's soul is, and it's not our job to judge—only God's. Let me tell you a story."

This woman, as it turned out, served on the church's bereavement team and used to think she always knew whether a person was going "up or down" when they died. But an experience while sitting at the deathbed of a man she hardly knew changed her perspective forever.

Sent to comfort a lonely, dying man, she held his hand during his last hours and read to him from the psalms. He told the woman he was an atheist, but she kept reading. Suddenly the man's eyes filled with tears. "My mother used to read that to me," he said when the caregiver got to Psalm 23. The familiar words, long forgotten but resurrected just in time, spoke to the man of the reality of a Savior.

The woman offered to pray with the man, but before she could, he called out the name of Jesus as he stared at someone or something only he could see. In the final moment of his life, faced with an eternity separated from God, he called on the only One who can save, and died a believer.

Like the thief on the cross, who called out to Jesus as he was dying, anyone may spend eternity in the presence of the Lord.

> *[God] says, "In the time of my favor I heard you, and in the day of salvation I helped you." I tell you, now is the time of God's favor, now is the day of salvation.*

2 CORINTHIANS 6:2

The Gilded Path

In a letter from Dr. Cabot: "[God] never makes mistakes. But He often deals far differently with His disciples. He lets them grope their way in the dark until they fully learn how blind they are, how helpless, how absolutely in need of Him. What His methods will be with you I cannot foretell. But you may be sure that He never works in an arbitrary way. He has a reason for everything He does. You may not understand why He leads you now in this way and now in that, but you may, nay, you must believe that perfection is stamped on His every act."

We all know people who seem to live a charmed life, filled with every type of blessing imaginable—a happy marriage, close family, financial prosperity, career satisfaction. Even their dog looks happy. And we wonder: What are they doing right that we haven't figured out yet? Is there some formula for the good life that we can tap into?

But God works with His children in very different ways and takes some by a short, direct route and others by the long, circuitous way. Some traipse down a seemingly gilded path, and others trudge a rocky, narrow road—uphill all the way. No doubt some of this depends on how we respond to our Father's promptings and whether we are quick to obey His leading or resist Him at every turn. But in God's economy there are no formulas or quick fixes, and we can be sure that even those who seem to have an easy ride go through their own times of testing.

There's also the indefinable element of God's purpose. Some of His children are destined to live quiet, simple lives, perhaps laying the groundwork for His future plan that will be fulfilled in another generation, through their children or their "spiritual children." Others have a calling that demands a long course of strenuous testing and preparation, for to whom much is given, much is expected.

Those, like Joseph, who are called to endure trials in preparation for God's ultimate purpose will have it very hard in the first part of their earthly journeys, but that is not the end of the story. These individuals are being prepared for greatness in the kingdom of God and require a training course that can stretch over decades.

Each of us must discover our divine purpose—what God has placed us here to do—and make every day count toward the fulfillment of that purpose.

Lead a life worthy of the calling
to which you have been called.

Ephesians 4:1 nrsv

Lukewarm Milk

In a letter from Dr. Cabot: "I beg you, my dear child, if you are doing this aimless, useless work, to stop short at once. Life is too precious to spend in a treadmill. Having been pardoned by your God and Savior, the next thing you have to do is to show your gratitude for this infinite favor by consecrating yourself entirely to Him, body, soul, and spirit. This is the least you can do. He has bought you with a price, and you are no longer your own."

When the apostle John recorded the book of Revelation, he penned words both curious and disturbing—namely that Jesus prefers us to be either "hot or cold" in our love for Him; those who are lukewarm He will spew out of His mouth.

At first reading, these sound like very harsh words. After all, isn't believing in Jesus and doing our Sunday best better than living a reprobate life? And what's so horrible about *lukewarm* anyway? But God sees things in a different light.

A pastor put it this way: "Think of a glass of milk. Milk is useful and *desirable* when it's either hot or cold. Cold milk is refreshing by itself and perfect with cereal. Hot milk, if you add a little cocoa powder to it, makes hot cocoa—or steaming oatmeal if you add it to a bowl of oat flakes. But nobody likes to drink lukewarm milk. Instead of drinking it, we put it in the cat's bowl."

Since God paid such a high price for our salvation—the ultimate price actually—He expects that when we accept His Son we will consecrate ourselves entirely to Him, body, soul, and spirit. Anything less is an insult to His sacrifice.

We get tripped up by thinking that we'll work harder. We'll pull ourselves up by our bootstraps and pray longer, go to church more often, do more good works. . . . But then we've only set our foot onto the "treadmill of striving" and trying to earn our salvation.

So what are we to do? We throw our hands up. . . . Why is the Christian walk so hard?

The secret is in the word of Dr. Cabot's letter: *consecrating*. Our part is to spend time with our Father and consecrate ourselves to His holy work in and through us; it is *His* job to transform us into the image of His Son.

> *Consecrate yourselves therefore, and be holy;*
> *for I am the LORD your God.*
>
> LEVITICUS 20:7 NRSV

Beautiful Imperfections

In a letter from Dr. Cabot: "'Can I not give myself so far to God as to feel a sweet sense of peace with Him, and be sure of final salvation, and yet, to a certain extent, indulge and gratify myself? If I give myself entirely away to Him and lose all ownership in myself, He may deny me many things I greatly desire. He may make my life hard and wearisome, depriving me of all that now makes it agreeable.' But, I reply, this is no matter of parley and discussion; it is not optional with God's children whether they will pay Him a part of the price they owe Him and keep back the rest."

On a trip to Colonial Williamsburg, a family visited the glassblowers' workshop. Dressed in the traditional Colonial garb, the glassblowers worked their craft using only the tools used in the eighteenth century.

The family's daughter, a girl of ten, watched as a glassblower picked up a pontil—a long metal rod attached to a glob of molten glass—and placed it on a battledore, a flat wooden paddle on which he rolled and shaped the molten glass. Next, using a hollow blowpipe, the artisan shaped the molten glob into a vase, literally breathing life into it. He used calipers to measure the emerging vase, pincers to stretch and squeeze the molten glass, and *pucellas* to twist and stretch it even more. The pincers helped the glassmaker create a pretty scalloped shape along the rim of the vase. When the vase finally reached the glassmaker's desired shape, he took shears and trimmed off the excess molten glass around the edges. Finally, the glassmaker placed the vase in a *lehr*, a special oven used to strengthen the glassware before it could be put to good use.

In awe, the girl asked for one special vase she had seen during the demonstration. As the clerk brought the vase down from the shelf, the little girl spotted a bubble in the glass. "It's not perfect," she said.

Her mother smiled. "I think that tiny bubble makes the vase unique. Look how it catches the light." She held the vase up and the little girl saw what her mother saw: beauty in imperfection, lovingly crafted by the artisan.

In the same way, God takes His time as He molds and shapes us, using our flaws to craft something ultimately so beautiful—so individual—that there will never be another one just like us.

> *"Before I formed you in the womb I knew you,*
> *and before you were born I consecrated you."*

JEREMIAH 1:5 NRSV

The Doctor Is In

In a letter from Dr. Cabot: "As soon as you become the Lord's by your own deliberate and conscious act, He will begin that process of sanctification, which is to make you holy as He is holy, perfect as He is perfect. He becomes at once your Physician as well as your dearest and best Friend, but He will use no painful remedy that can be avoided. Remember that it is His will that you should be sanctified and that the work of making you holy is His, not yours. At the same time you are not to sit with folded hands, waiting for this blessing. You are to avoid laying hindrances in His way, and you are to exercise faith in Him as just as able and just as willing to give you sanctification as He was to give you redemption."

For decades cartoonist Charles Schulz kept us smiling as we watched the antics of a group of little kids known as the Peanuts gang. The unlikely hero, Charlie Brown, endured insults and gags from his neighborhood playmates, but he also found love and meaning.

Often when Charlie needed advice he visited Lucy's "psychiatric booth," which was marked by a sign that read: THE DOCTOR IS IN. Fortunately for Charlie, his "frenemy" Lucy always had the right prescription for whatever he needed, and the cartoon saga went on—both bittersweet and happy.

Our own lives are much more fraught with upheaval and

uncertainty, and human beings don't always get the "happily ever after"—or, as is the case in Peanuts, even a touching bit of closure. What we do have is reality, purpose, destiny, and immortality. And of course our very own Physician.

The prophet Isaiah said that Jesus binds up the broken-hearted and sets those bound by sin free. And the psalmist David tells us that God restores our souls. Once we are born again, our journey has only just begun and the work of sanctification begins. Here is where our loving Physician steps forward, pouring a healing balm onto our wounds and binding us up little by little, year after year, until one day our wounds are only faint scars—healed over but still there to remind us of how far we've come, how far He's brought us, so that we in turn may help to heal others.

"For you who revere my name, the sun of righteousness will rise with healing in its rays. And you will go out and frolic like well-fed calves."

MALACHI 4:2

Power in a Word

In a letter from Dr. Cabot: "In reading the Bible I advise you to choose detached passages, or even one verse a day, rather than whole chapters. Study every word; ponder and pray over it till you have got from it all the truth it contains."

The Word of God is a living text, filled with the very life force of the Creator and able to speak to our lives in ways we cannot imagine and sometimes least expect. If we spend any amount of time in those pages, we will undoubtedly have our own "*rhema* moments"—times when the words of scripture seem to leap off the page and into our hearts, speaking a truth that transforms us profoundly.

Rhema literally means an "utterance" or "thing said" in Greek. While both the Greek words *rhema* and *logos* translate to the English *word*, there is a distinction in the original Greek. *Rhema* refers to what Christ says, while *logos* refers to Christ Himself.

On the night of Jesus' betrayal—the night of the Last Supper—Jesus was gathered with His twelve disciples in an upper room to observe the Passover. He told the disciples He was about to return to His Father, but in the midst of their confusion and alarm, He gave them a wonderful promise: after

He departs, He will send a Helper, a Comforter—the Holy Spirit—who will teach them and help them remember what He has said to them. What an amazing night that must have been! It makes us wonder how it felt to literally sit at Jesus' feet.

This conversation Jesus had with His disciples must be why some modern-day Christians debate who had it easier: the believers who walked and talked with Jesus, the Son of God in the flesh, or we who live two hundred centuries later. But Jesus Himself answered this question, and many may find what He said surprising. Jesus told His followers: "It is better for you that I go away" (John 16:7 NCV), because until He left the Holy Spirit could not come.

First-century believers before Christ's resurrection had to be in His physical presence to hear the words of God, or go to the temple to hear the scriptures read. We are privileged to have the indwelling Spirit of God *live in our hearts and speak to us one-on-one.*

> *[Jesus said,] "The Helper will teach you everything and will cause you to remember all that I told you. This Helper is the Holy Spirit whom the Father will send in my name."*
>
> JOHN 14:26 NCV

The Road to Emmaus

In a letter from Dr. Cabot: "You cannot will to possess the spirit of Christ; that must come as His gift; but you can choose to study His life and to imitate it. This will infallibly lead to such self-denying work as visiting the poor, nursing the sick, giving of your time and money to the needy, and the like. If the thought of such self-denial is repugnant to you, remember that it is enough for the disciple to be as his Lord. And let me assure you that as you penetrate the labyrinth of life in pursuit of Christian duty, you will often be surprised and charmed by meeting your Master Himself amid its windings and turnings and receive His soul-inspiring smile. Or, I should rather say, you will always meet Him, wherever you go."

Imagine for a moment—Jerusalem is in an uproar. It has been three days since the prophet from Nazareth who claimed He was the Son of God died alongside two common criminals. Shell-shocked from the events, two of Jesus' followers decide to make the seven-mile walk to Emmaus, a nearby village. As they walk along, somberly discussing the events of the past few days, a stranger comes up, falls into step with them, and asks what events they are talking about.

"Are you the only stranger in Jerusalem? Do you mean to say you honestly don't know what has happened over the last few days?" says one guy, incredulous.

The resurrected Jesus talks to them about Himself, assuring them that all the events had to happen according to scripture, but He veils their eyes so they do not recognize Him. Later, they persuade this "stranger" to dine with them in Emmaus, and as He sits at the table with them, Jesus does something He had done so many times in their midst: He takes the bread, blesses it, and then breaks it to share with them. At that moment, "their eyes were opened and they knew Him" (Luke 24:31 NKJV).

"Didn't our hearts burn within us as He spoke on the road to Emmaus!" they exclaim with the clarity of hindsight.

As we journey through our own lives, we, too, are blessed to "meet Jesus"—or rather, He meets us. We might not always recognize Him at first. But if we are listening, our hearts will begin to burn within us as well.

> *[Jesus] said, "I am the light of the world. Whoever follows me will never walk in darkness, but will have the light of life."*
>
> JOHN 8:12

Staying in the Flow

" 'Oh, I do wish,' I cried, 'that God had given us plain rules about which we could make no mistake.' 'I think His rules are plain,' [Mother] replied. 'And some liberty of action He must leave us or we should become mere machines. I think that those who love Him and wait upon Him day by day learn His will almost imperceptibly and need not go astray.' "

In the animated movie *Finding Nemo*, the title character's friends go on an undersea voyage to rescue their clown fish buddy. At first they struggle to swim in the vast ocean, and they encounter schools of fish and other obstacles to their speedy progress. Then along comes a sea turtle who teaches them a valuable lesson: if they jump into the flow of the East Australian Current, they will be swept along faster than they ever dreamed possible—and certainly faster than they could ever swim on their own. The sea creatures who hitch a ride in the "EAC" have discovered the Concorde jet of undersea travel, and it makes all the difference.

In this amusing story we can see a parallel to our own lives as believers. We come to Christ as spiritual neophytes, babies where the things of God are concerned. Then we grow up a bit and learn a few things—the Father is stretching us out of our comfort zones and demanding more of us.

But sooner or later we hit a wall, and for many of us it feels as if we're traveling at a pace of two steps forward, three steps back. What we need is a spiritual EAC, a means of flowing in the things of God under the power of something greater than ourselves.

That *something* is actually a *someone*—the Holy Spirit, and we are hardwired spiritually to receive His indwelling power the moment we are born again. The New Testament writers (and Jesus Himself) spoke of the importance of the Holy Spirit in the life of a believer. And therein lies the secret: we were never intended to "do" Christianity on our own; in fact we can't. *But God* supplied the answer, and He keeps on supplying it every day, like fresh manna in the wilderness. No matter what our struggle is, no matter what we're facing, the answer is always "but God."

What we have received is not the spirit of the world, but the Spirit who is from God, so that we may understand what God has freely given us.

1 Corinthians 2:12

Finding True North

"Mother sees that I am restless and out of sorts. 'What is it, dear?' she asked this morning. 'Has Dr. Elliott anything to do with the unsettled state you are in?' 'Why, no, Mother,' I answered. 'My going away has broken up all my habits; that's all. Still, if I knew Dr. Elliott did not care much and was beginning to forget it, I dare say I should feel better.' 'If you were perfectly sure that you never could return his affection,' she said, 'you were quite right in telling him so at once. But if you had any misgivings on the subject, it would have been better to wait and ask God to direct you.'"

Because of the earth's gravitational pull, a compass can steer us toward our intended destinations, even saving lives on occasion. This simple tool with a spinning arrow and designations for north, south, east, and west will always find true north. The compass's inner workings are designed to point in a northerly direction regardless of climate, weather, altitude, latitude, and topographical changes.

God designed us with ingenious inner workings as well. Christian philosopher Blaise Pascal said that our Maker designed His prize creation with "a God-shaped vacuum in the heart of every man." Our souls are inclined to find a spiritual true north, and that place of safety and direction is God Himself.

Our heavenly Father is a feeling God—a God of infinite love—and for that reason He saw fit to create us with the ability to respond to His love of our own free will. Conversely, we can choose to reject His love, but if we do our "compass" will always be spinning, searching desperately for true north.

A malfunctioning compass is worthless to a traveler. He or she would be better off guiding their progress by the stars. Likewise, those who reject God's invitation to commune with Him will resort to other means to navigate this earthly life, and they may get by for a while—even appear successful in their self-navigation. But eventually they will reach a place where the God-shaped hole in their hearts gapes so wide it can no longer be filled with anything, or anyone, other than the Creator, who is always patiently waiting to draw them back to Himself.

To choose life is to love the LORD your God,
obey him, and stay close to him. He is your life.

DEUTERONOMY 30:20 NCV

The Sweetest Peace

"I am not going to sit down in sentimental despondency to weep over this irreparable past. No human being could forgive such folly as mine; but God can. In my sorrowfulness and loneliness I fly to Him and find what is better than earthly felicity, the sweetest peace. He allowed me to bring upon myself, in one hasty moment, a shadow out of which I shall not soon pass; but He pities and He forgives me, and I have had many precious moments when I could say sincerely and joyfully, 'Whom have I in heaven but thee? and there is none upon earth that I desire beside thee' (Psalm 73:25)."

A small congregation in a bustling Southern city decided to go outside the walls of the church and actually *be* the church in the New Testament sense—reaching out to people who had been sidelined by society, including the homeless.

One man in particular, a nearly toothless man named Frankie, found a warm spot in the hearts of the people and started showing up for Sunday services and other events. He always wore the same clothes: tattered jeans stiff with accumulated dirt, an oversized shirt, and a green army jacket. Sensing he was accepted rather than rejected, he hung around even more often.

As time went by, the people noticed that Frankie smiled more—gap-toothed and all. Someone paid for him to stay at a halfway house so he could get cleaned up and have a bed each night. His clothes got washed and he no longer smelled, but the biggest change was his expression.

Frankie was a different man. Listening to God's Word week after week effected a change in this formerly shiftless man who literally had nowhere to go. The Sunday a parishioner offered him a part-time job doing landscaping work, he left the church building a foot taller than he'd walked in it.

One week a young man at the church fell into conversation with Frankie, and what he heard touched him to his soul: "I don't know what it is," Frankie said, shaking his head, "but I step in this place, I feel all warm inside. . .like nothing I ever felt before. Better than any high I know of."

The young man smiled. "That's the love and peace of God. And the more time you spend with Him, the thicker it grows."

God's love and peace are literal catalysts of change that can motivate even the most discouraged and hardened soul.

Grace, mercy and peace from God the Father and from Jesus Christ, the Father's Son, will be with us in truth and love.

2 JOHN 1:3

Fence-Sitting

"The last day of the very happiest summer I ever spent. If I had only been willing to believe the testimony of others I might have been just as happy long ago. But I wanted to have all there was in God and all there was in the world at once; and there was a constant, painful struggle between the two. I hope that struggle is now over. I deliberately choose and prefer God. I have found a sweet peace in trying to please Him such as I never conceived of. I would not change it for all the best things this world can give."

Some fledgling Christians hit the ground running, casting in their lots with Jesus and never looking back. They are the ones who become the front-runners, God's champions in the long footrace of faith.

Other believers make a great start but lose confidence in their new faith—or run out of steam, or cave in to the pressure to conform to the world around them. And some simply get distracted and never put foot to pavement when the starting gun fires off.

Lastly is the group of "fence-sitters"; we may even be among them ourselves. They are so in love with Jesus and ready to commit their all to Him—almost. They'll get around to it eventually, but first they need to achieve worldly success or experience a few sensual pleasures. This life is so short, and they don't want to leave any stone unturned. But anyone who straddles the fence is likely to miss opportunities on either side. God has strong words for any of us who settle for indecision. In essence, He says, "Choose your side—you can't serve others and Me, too."

When a rich young ruler came to Jesus desiring to follow Him, Jesus already knew the state of his heart. He knew this young man was ready to do whatever it took to follow Him—except the one thing that mattered most in his case. Since "riches" had a hold on the young man's heart, that was the area Jesus required him to surrender, never looking back.

Mark's Gospel tells us the young man "went away sad" because he couldn't do it. He couldn't slide off the fence and follow hard after Jesus. It may not be riches that keep some of us on the fence. Whatever it is, let's determine to go away glad!

It is the LORD your God you must follow, and him you must revere. Keep his commands and obey him; serve him and hold fast to him.

DEUTERONOMY 13:4

Being Schooled

"I have a great deal to learn. I am like a child who cannot run to get what he wants but approaches it step by step, slowly, timidly— and yet approaches it. I am amazed at the patience of my blessed Master and Teacher, but how I love His school!"

A young man named Augustine frolicked through his early life in the fourth century, sampling all the world's pleasures—not the least of which was women. Leading a life of debauchery, he threw off the teachings of his Christian mother and dove headfirst into the good life. This is the man who prayed the famous prayer, "[Lord,] Grant me chastity and continence, but not yet."

Young men of his time were not much different from young men today. They traded stories about their exploits with women and even made them up when they lacked actual experiences. Always out to have a good time, Augustine fell right in step with his peers.

In the summer of 386, still in his early thirties, Augustine was deeply moved and inspired by the story of one of the "Desert Fathers," Saint Anthony. Something stirred within his heart, and a voice in his spirit told him to *"take up and read"*—which he took to be a divine command to pick up the scriptures and read. He read the first thing his eyes fell upon, Paul's epistle to the Romans, chapters 12 through 15, a section that talks about the transformation of believers.

Having already obtained a brilliant education, Augustine now undertook a rigorous "school of discipleship" and eventually became one of the most revered theologians of his time—and remains such even to this day.

God takes each of us through our own customized course of spiritual growth, with Christ our example and the Holy Spirit our Teacher. His curriculum is the same—the Word of God—yet through supernatural intervention it is unique to each individual believer so that one person's "school" will be different from another's.

How long do we stay in this school of discipleship? All our earthly lives. Some of us advance quickly and grow by leaps and bounds; others are like late-blooming flowers that finally bear fruit on the tree. The good news is if we remain in His school—we will all eventually graduate.

Jesus said to his disciples, "Whoever wants to be my disciple must deny themselves and take up their cross and follow me."

MATTHEW 16:24–25

The Ministry of Disappointment

"[Dr. Elliott] then made a little address on the ministry of disappointment, as he called it. He spoke so cheerfully and hopefully that I began to see, almost for the first time, God's reason for the petty trials and crosses that help to make up every day of one's life. He said there were few who were not constantly disappointed with themselves, with their slow progress, their childishness and weakness; disappointed with their friends who, strangely enough, were never quite perfect enough; and disappointed with the world, which was always promising so much and giving so little. Then he urged a wise and patient consent to this discipline, which, if rightly used, would help to temper and strengthen the soul against the day of sorrow and bereavement."

Joseph—the one famed for his multicolored coat—goes from brash teenager to prime minister of Egypt in the span of more than fourteen hard years. At times he must have been nearly crushed with disappointment. Yet through it all, God kept Joseph for a very special purpose.

It all started with a stunning prophetic dream in which a teenaged Joseph metaphorically saw his parents and eleven brothers bowing down to him. A second dream confirmed it. His heart must have pounded with excitement as he ran to tell his family. God meant him for greatness!

His family, especially his brothers, did not receive the

news with the jubilance Joseph expected. In fact, the jealous brothers plotted his death, but instead sold him to a caravan of Ishmaelite traders.

Joseph's life—though it started with a prophetic promise and a clear call—went from bad to worse. Sold at auction in Egypt, he soon became a trusted household administrator. Just when things were looking brighter, Joseph caught the wandering eye of the boss's wife. When Joseph refused her advances, she falsely accused him of rape, and he was cast into prison.

Eventually his God-given gift of interpreting dreams becomes his "get out of jail free" card, and Joseph was promoted to Pharaoh's right-hand man—assigned with the task of overseeing the storage and rationing of grain for a coming famine. Here at last we see his divine purpose played out. The truly amazing thing is that Joseph *recognized* God's hand on his life, even in the midst of his years of suffering and disappointment.

God is watching us during our hard times to see how we will react. Will we become bitter or better during our "ministry of disappointment"?

God is faithful, and he will not let you be tested beyond
your strength, but with the testing he will also provide
the way out so that you may be able to endure it.

1 CORINTHIANS 10:13 NRSV

Love's Courageous Act

"Oh, how glad I am that God has cast in my lot with a man whose whole business is to minister to others! I am sure this will, of itself, keep him unworldly and unselfish. How delicious it is to love such a character, and how happy I shall be to go with him to sickrooms and to dying beds! He has already taught me that lessons learned in such scenes far outweigh in value what books and sermons, even, can teach. . . . How good God has been to me! I do hope and pray that this new, this absorbing love has not detached my soul from Him, will not detach it. If I knew it would, could I, should I have courage to cut it off and cast it from me?"

Like any loving parent, God enjoys giving good gifts to His children. He even saves the very best for them, though they may have to wait for it. Yet, after years of disappointments, a peculiar thing can take place in our hearts. Even as we petition God to fulfill our heart's desire—according to His will—we may actually feel guilty for wanting this "good thing" He promised.

That's not to say He allows us to place any person or thing above Him; He doesn't. Our God is a jealous God who pursues us with the zeal of a romance. And He longs for us to return His love on our own, without being prompted, without being "forced" into it.

What good is a love relationship where one partner does all the loving and the other shrugs and says "whatever"?

Knowing our Father is so jealous for our hearts, we wonder how He can share us with another human being. But there in the words of Genesis 2 we see that *love* is what drove Him to create a suitable helpmate for Adam.

It's said that the truest test of a relationship (spiritually speaking) is whether the person you're with draws you closer to the Lord or further from Him. When God sends the right one, the pieces fall into place and everything "fits." God may choose to test our love for Him by requiring us to place that special man or woman at His feet, so to speak—offering back to Him what He gave to us. But if God brings them back, we know our puzzle is complete at last.

> *[Jesus spoke, saying]: "It is your Father's good pleasure to give you the kingdom."*
>
> LUKE 12:32 NKJV

Three-Stranded Cord

"Before I give myself to Ernest and before I leave home forever, I may once more give myself away to God. I have been too much absorbed in my earthly love and am shocked to find how it fills my thoughts. But I will belong to God. I will begin my married life in His fear, depending on Him to make me an unselfish, devoted wife."

A cord of three strands is not quickly broken" (Ecclesiastes 4:12), wrote Solomon, the wise king of ancient Israel. Today, millennia after he penned those words, the three-stranded-cord metaphor still finds its way into many wedding ceremonies.

The proverb's meaning is clear: a man and woman together is a good thing, but a man, a woman, and God is a divine thing. The wear and tear of time and daily living has a way of dulling the shine of even the most enchanting love story, and what started as a "forever love" can diminish into resentment and bitterness and a never-ending blame game.

But when two people are hemmed in by God's love and their union is bolstered by His strength, they have found the key to making it through the hard times as well as the good times. Why? Because when they falter and can't go on in their own strength, God is with them saying, "I'm here. Let Me love through you. Let Me help you in this. Let Me be your Rock, your hiding place, your strong tower."

Marriage has a bad reputation in our modern culture. One in two marriages ends in divorce, and many believe it's easier just to live together and "take him for a test drive" or "see how she meshes with my life." Everything is centered on protecting the almighty *self* first, and then maybe, perhaps, seeing if the other person meets all our needs and requirements.

What happened to the beauty of the garden union, where God prepares one special woman for one special man and lovingly presents her to him—his "suitable helpmate"—and they become one flesh?

Those of us who would follow hard after God know we dare not give ourselves to another until we've given ourselves—body, soul, mind, and strength—to our Father first. If we get that part right, our love story's ending should be as joyful as its beginning.

Though one may be overpowered, two can defend themselves.
A cord of three strands is not quickly broken.

ECCLESIASTES 4:12

Twain Hearts, One Life

"What is married life? An occasional meeting, a kiss here and a caress there? Or is it the sacred union of the twain who walk together side by side, knowing each other's joys and sorrows and going Heavenward hand in hand?"

The first time the young woman witnessed her coworker's marriage in action, it floored her. She'd never seen a husband and wife cherish each other the way these two did. Their little kindnesses added up to a big "I LOVE YOU" spelled out in actions rather than just words.

Her own sad marriage had ended in divorce, and as she observed her friend, she took note of the myriad ways her marriage flourished—well beyond the thirty-year mark.

"Hey, do you want to join us for lunch?" the young woman asked her friend. "A bunch of us are going out to Chili's."

"Nah, you go ahead," the older woman answered, a twinkle in her eye. "My husband is coming home from his trip tonight, and I want to prepare his favorite dinner. I need to run to the grocery store."

The young woman shrugged. "Okay, but if you change your mind you know where to find us." She smiled as she left the office with a few other coworkers.

Later that afternoon, a huge bouquet of flowers arrived at the office for her friend—with a note that read: "Just because I love you. See you tonight." *Smart man*, she thought.

Two weeks later, the whole office gang went out to eat, and as they came into the restaurant the older woman spied her husband eating with a client. "Oh, look, there's my sweetie," she said, waving discreetly in his direction so as not to disturb what looked like an important business lunch.

The older woman's husband made his way over to the table before he left, set a handful of mints in front of her, and whispered in her ear "for my bride." He brushed her cheek with a kiss and then left to meet up with his client. The young woman never forgot the look on her coworker's face. Here was a woman cherished and a husband beloved, she thought.

Perfect marriages don't exist. We all experience bumps, challenges, and even an occasional crisis. But the union of two people who love God and love each other is beautiful to see and definitely something to strive for.

Each man should have his own wife
and each woman her own husband.

1 CORINTHIANS 7:2 NRSV

Living Beautifully

"'Speaking beautifully is little to the purpose unless one lives beautifully,' [Ernest] said sadly. 'And how is it possible that you and I, a Christian man and a Christian woman, are going on and on with such scenes as this? Are you to wear your life out because I have not your frantic way of loving, and am I to be made weary of mine because I cannot satisfy you?' 'But, Ernest,' I said, 'you used to satisfy me! Oh, how happy I was in those first days when we were always together and you seemed so fond of me!' I was down on the floor by this time and looking up into his pale, anxious face. 'Dear child,' he said, 'I do love you, and that more than you know. But you would not have me leave my work and spend my whole time telling you so?'"

Saint Francis of Assisi is erroneously credited with the famous quote "Preach the Gospel at all times. Use words if necessary." While scholars have proved that none of his writings contain this actual quote, the closest they can come is wording found in the rules on how the monks of the Franciscan order should go about preaching.

Francis's first biographer, Thomas of Celano, painted a picture of a man who preached—using words—quite passionately—sometimes in as many as five villages a day, often outdoors. When in the country, he would preach from a granary doorway or the top of a bale of straw. In town, he would stand on a box or the steps of a public building. The strange little preacher from Assisi drew listeners with his fiery speech and dancing feet.

The simple truth seems to be a marriage of both words and deeds, for Francis's legacy of peacemaking, his fervor for preaching the Gospel, and his love for creation remain relevant today, eight hundred years after he lived.

When all is said and done, if we want a credible testimony, what we say must line up with what we do as representatives of Christ. No wonder the apostle Paul said we are "living letters" read of all men. People are watching our lives—watching to see if Jesus makes any difference in the lives of flawed human beings. They are watching to see if we "live beautifully," not just speak pretty Christianese.

"How beautiful are the feet of those who preach the gospel of peace, who bring glad tidings of good things!"

ROMANS 10:15 NKJV

Marriage "Felicity"

"I was begging and beseeching God not to let us drift apart, not to let us lose one jot or tittle of our love for each other, to enable me to understand my dear, dear husband and make him understand me."

Jane Austen wrote stories that always ended in a happy romance and a marriage of "felicity," a word we seldom use today but one rife with meaning. Simply put, felicity is the quality or state of being happy—great happiness—what we expect when the bride and groom, hand in hand, dash off to their waiting limo, eager to begin a life of married bliss.

It certainly seems obvious that God designed man and woman to live in perfect equality and harmony, in a state of felicity to the *n*th degree. But anyone who has been married knows this was before human frailty—sin—entered the garden in the form of a lie from Satan. Once that cataclysmic event took place, human relations were forever tainted. Amidst the complexity of modern marriages, one thing sets apart those with *felicity*: mutual understanding.

But the apostle Paul—himself a happy bachelor—took things a step further and advised married men and women thus: the men were admonished to *love* their wives, the wives to *respect* their husbands. Isn't it interesting that one sex is commanded to love and the other to respect?

If we take scripture to be God-breathed, then we know the real author is God Himself, writing through human hands. And He must have known the core issue for men is to be respected, while the deepest need of a woman is to be loved. Unfortunately, in our human fog, we assume that our mate needs what we need—the result being that no one is very happy at all!

Finding felicity in marriage requires a reprogramming of the human mind and a selfless investment in learning what pleases others. God has given us the insights we need in His Word, but they only bring understanding when both husband and wife submit to the instruction of the Holy Spirit.

Felicity is God's best for every marriage. It takes commitment, patience, and love, but it is doable, and the joy it brings is worth whatever it may take to get there.

Greet one another with a kiss of love.

1 PETER 5:14 NRSV

Root-Cellar Sins

"Let me think what I really and truly most want now. First of all, then, if God should speak to me at this moment and offer to give just one thing and that alone, I should say without hesitation, Love to Thee, O my Master! Next to that, if I could have one thing more, I would choose to be a thoroughly unselfish, devoted wife. Down in my secret heart I know there lurks another wish, which I am ashamed of."

We all struggle with them, and we all try to forget they're there—those character flaws and downright *bad* traits that lurk in the basements of our spiritual "houses." We can walk into church with our scrubbed faces and pressed clothes, smiling and looking godly, but deep in our hearts is a seed of bitterness or resentment or jealousy or envy or pride.

When we first come to Christ, He purges away all our surface sins, the outer trappings of ungodliness that mark us as unbelievers to a watching world. But as the years go by, if we stay on the path of faith, God takes a crowbar and begins to pry up the floorboards, exposing all the hidden sins we so carefully tucked away—out of sight, maybe even out of mind.

He doesn't do this to be cruel but rather to make us righteous, to make us more like Him. And He works with a steady but gentle hand, loving us too much to leave us like

Snow White's fateful apple: shiny and red on the outside, but poisonous on the inside.

One of the surest tests of how much we've matured in the Lord is the way we behave under pressure, uncomfortable circumstances, or around people we don't like. Our Father leaves nothing out. In the long work of sanctification—the lifetime process of sanding down our rough edges—He addresses one area after another. And like any good teacher, He will test us and require that we *pass* the test in one area before graduating us to deal with the next.

If we fail the test, guess what happens? We get to take it again. . .and again. . .and again until we finally get an A. Little wonder that Jesus told His followers to "count the cost" (Luke 14:28 NKJV) before signing on to be a Christian. The walk of faith is not for the fainthearted to be sure, but let us also not forget the "joy unspeakable" (1 Peter 1:8 KJV) that belongs to those who believe.

> *Whoever conceals their sins does not prosper, but the one who confesses and renounces them finds mercy.*

> PROVERBS 28:13

Dangerous Prayers

"If God chooses quite another lot for you, you may be sure that He sees that you need something totally different from what you want. You said just now that you would gladly go through any trial in order to attain a personal love for Christ that should become the ruling principle of your life. Now as soon as God sees this desire in you, is He not king, is He not wise in appointing such trials as He knows will lead to this end?"

A common adage warns, "Be careful what you pray for—you just might get it." If ever there was a dangerous prayer, it's one in which we ask God to test us or to give us patience.

In the flare of spiritual passion, we may toss grandiose words up to heaven, making promises we can't keep and brashly declaring, like the disciple Peter, that we will never forsake our Lord. And, like Peter, we may be humiliated to find out just how frail and human we are.

On the night of Jesus' betrayal, as He predicted that one among the twelve disciples would turn Him over to the temple authorities, Peter loudly proclaimed that he would follow His Lord anywhere, even if it meant his own death. Jesus' eyes must have clouded with sorrow as He gazed at Peter, His beloved first disciple, and calmly informed him that he would indeed deny Him—sooner rather than later.

If we were in Peter's shoes, we probably would have reacted the same way he did: "You must be mistaken, Lord, not us. We're the ones who love You, remember? Now give us some test that we may prove our love for You."

But the rooster crowed and Peter realized to his horror that Jesus had been right. In the heat of the moment, fearing for his life, he denied his Lord three times and then wept bitterly. Later in the story, after His resurrection, Jesus lovingly restored this bold, brash fisherman—now a fisher of men—with words of reassurance and acceptance. And Peter was never the same man again.

Peter learned a hard lesson that night, and we are wise to learn from his example rather than to fall into the same pit of self-sufficiency and pride. God is not impressed with our spiritual bravado or our proclamations; He is moved by our obedience and the wisdom to pray: "Your grace is sufficient for me."

In your love you kept me from the pit of destruction;
you have put all my sins behind your back.

ISAIAH 38:17

Running to God

" 'We look at our fellow men too much from the standpoint of our own prejudices. They may be wrong, they may have their faults and foibles, and they may call out all the meanest and most hateful in us. But they are not all wrong; they have their virtues, and when they excite our bad passions by their own, they may be as ashamed and sorry as we are irritated. And I think some of the best, most contrite, most useful of men and women, whose prayers prevail with God and bring down blessings into the homes in which they dwell, often possess unlovely traits that furnish them with their best discipline. The very fact that they are ashamed of themselves drives them to God; they feel safe in His presence. And while they lie in the very dust of self-confusion at His feet, they are dear to Him and have power with Him.' "

When we hear the phrase "follow hard after God," we often zero in on the "hard" part and think, *If I just try harder, if I do more ministry, if I read my Bible more and spend more time in prayer, God will be pleased with me.* We are forever getting tripped up by the false notion that we have to earn God's love and grace and forgiveness.

In reality, it is our total reliance upon God that frees us from our clubfooted struggle along the rocky path of life. When we free-fall into His arms—and His grace—placing all our dependence on Him, our clunky feet are transformed into graceful feet that can run along behind the Shepherd wherever He may take us.

There are two kinds of Christians: those who run away from God when they mess up and sin horribly, and those who run *to Him*. Our human nature automatically shrinks from getting in trouble with authority. None of us likes that guilty feeling. So what separates the second type of believer from the first?

The answer is found in the heart. When we truly regard God as our Father—our Daddy—we know how much He loves us, and we feel cherished and protected in that love. Perfect love casts out all fear. So when we trip and fall, we let Him help us to our feet, dust us off, and lead the way back up the mountain again.

The Sovereign LORD is my strength; he makes my feet like the feet of a deer, he enables me to tread on the heights.

HABAKKUK 3:19

Less Is More

"I have just been to see Mrs. Campbell. In answer to my routine lamentations, she took up a book and read me what was called, as nearly as I can remember, 'Four steps that lead to peace.' 'Be desirous of doing the will of another, rather than thine own.' 'Choose always to have less, rather than more.' 'Seek always the lowest place, and to be inferior to every one.' 'Wish always, and pray, that the will of God may be wholly fulfilled in thee.'"

Needing a break from the rat race and a place to recharge his creative batteries, a man took a trip to a spiritual retreat in rural Georgia. Recommended by his good friend, the retreat was operated by a woman who had devoted herself to the ascetic life and then realized others needed what she'd found among the gently rolling terrain of the countryside. Each room of the guesthouse was spartan but comfortable, with a view of the woods that bordered the property. The food was simple, organic fare prepared without sauces. The retreat recognized a "code of silence," and even shared meals were taken in silence around the table. A bell called any who wanted to participate to the daily evening prayer service.

Something happened as the man let the cares of the workaday world drop off him hour by silent hour. Encouraged to focus on God during their silent stay, the handful of guests appeared changed by the week's end. Faces looked more relaxed, eyes shone with an inner radiance, and when the guests spoke at last upon leaving the retreat, almost everyone had a tale to tell. As they turned inward, listening for the voice of the Holy Spirit, He spoke to them.

Few of us are called to the cloistered life, but every now and then—whether we travel to some distant location or take a quiet "stay-cation" at home—we need to recharge spiritually and remember that it's the simple things that make all the difference. These are a few of the principles we might all want to meditate on:

- We should seek to help others rather than ourselves.
- We should choose always to have less rather than more.
- We should let God and others promote us in due time—not ourselves.
- We should pray that God's will shall be fulfilled in our lives.

Thus says the Lord God. . .
"In quietness and confidence shall be your strength."

ISAIAH 30:15 NKJV

Learning Christ

*"'My dear,' [Mrs. Campbell] said with much tenderness and feeling,
'then the first thing you have to do is to learn Christ.' 'But how?'
'On your knees, my child, on your knees!' She was tired,
and I came away; and I have indeed been on my knees."*

In Greek mythology, Oedipus outwits the Sphinx that guards the gate to the city of Thebes by correctly answering the Sphinx's riddle: "Which creature has one voice and yet becomes four-footed and two-footed and three-footed?" A fearsome creature, the Sphinx was said to devour anyone unable to answer. But Oedipus solves the riddle by answering: "Man—who crawls on all fours as a baby, then walks on two feet as an adult, and then uses a walking stick in old age."

The elderly man hobbles along with a cane; the man in his prime strides upright, taking strong sure steps; but the baby crawls on his knees, humble and dependent. Isn't it interesting that Jesus said when we come to Him we must come as little children? Otherwise we have no hope of entering the kingdom of God.

We want to stride fully into the kingdom of heaven, wielding our talents and gifts like broadswords, showing God and others what we are made of. And yet Jesus says, "No, you must become like this little child," as He takes one up onto His lap.

Indeed, on our knees is exactly where the work of "learning Christ" is done—like babies, like infants taking milk, then growing sturdy enough to swallow whole food. Our loving Father monitors our growth and notices when we are ready to take our first halting steps. He delights to see us grow stronger, desiring the meat of His Word and not just pablum anymore. Soon we start to toddle, and then to run.

Even though we enter the kingdom of God as children, our Lord doesn't want us to remain immature spiritually. There's a big difference between being "childlike" and being "childish." A man or woman who stays childlike in heart is a wonderful example of God's influence; a man or woman who is *childish*— long after they grow into adulthood—is an embarrassment to all. If we stay on our knees, we can be assured of the former and steer clear of the latter.

As newborn babes, desire the pure milk
of the word, that you may grow.

1 PETER 2:2 NKJV

Soldiering On

"I think that I do begin, dimly it is true, but really, to understand that this terrible work that I was trying to do myself is Christ's work and must be done and will be done by Him. I take some pleasure in the thought and wonder why it has all this time been hidden from me, especially after what Dr. C. said in his letter. But I get hold of this idea in a misty, unsatisfactory way. If Christ is to do all, what am I to do? And have I not been told over and over again that the Christian life is one of conflict and that I am to fight like a good soldier?"

Some new Christians are alarmed to find out they've just enlisted as soldiers in a war that won't end until they leave this earth and fly to heaven. Jesus warned His followers throughout His three-year ministry not to join His army lightly. He urged them to "count the cost" and comprehend in a clear-headed way just what they were signing on for. Jesus took discipleship seriously; He even threw curveballs at would-be followers, making sure their hearts were in the right place if they intended to stay.

John the Beloved, in his Gospel, records a disturbing event. He writes that Jesus proclaimed Himself the bread that came down from heaven. He told them that unlike their forefathers who ate manna in the wilderness and died, whoever eats this bread will live forever.

Jesus made these remarks to a group of Jews who from the cradle had been taught all the scriptures and traditions of Judaism. The story of Moses leading the Hebrew children out of Egypt was sacred to them—so much so that one of their chief feasts, Passover, centered on this miraculous tale.

Who was this wandering Nazarene who proclaimed Himself the bread that came down from heaven? This sounded blasphemous to their Jewish ears. John tells us that many of Christ's followers were unable to accept His remarks and were offended by them.

God is not interested in our being pew-warmers or cheerleaders for church building fund-raisers. He doesn't want greeters in Christian country clubs. He wants us all in—body, soul, mind, and strength—or not at all. Joining His army is a high calling, for sure, but those who hear His invitation in their hearts would have it no other way.

Jesus declared, "I am the bread of life. Whoever comes to me will never go hungry, and whoever believes in me will never be thirsty."

JOHN 6:35

Prayer Power

"'It is my belief,' replied Dr. Cabot, 'that every prayer offered in the name of Jesus is sure to have its answer. Every such prayer is dictated by the Holy Spirit and therefore finds acceptance with God; and if your cry for mercy on poor Susan's soul did not prevail with Him in her behalf, as we may hope it did, then He has answered it in some other way.' These words impressed me very much. To think that every one of my poor prayers is answered! Every one!"

Prayer is one-to-one communion with our Father, yet we often treat it as a secret punch-code to a divine vending machine. Most of us can relate to falling on our knees only to whip out our long list of requests—never bothering to hear God speak back.

Have we ever stopped to think about the *power* and *privilege* of prayer? We are privileged to talk to the Creator of the universe! Not only does He ask us to pray, but He also longs for it. And in that private space with our Lord, something supernatural happens: angels are sent on assignment, solutions to problems drop into our minds, divine appointments are set in motion, provision appears out of nowhere, and people are healed.

But what about those times when our prayers aren't

answered? What then? The apostle James wrote that we don't receive because we fail to ask, and sometimes when we do ask we "ask amiss"—that is, ask for something or *someone* just so that we can fulfill a lustful desire in our hearts.

Thankfully, Jesus Himself taught us how to pray in the Lord's Prayer. His disciples, like us, needed a blueprint for how to talk to God, and Jesus was happy to comply. We open with heartfelt praise and declare that His works be established in the earth; next we bring Him our daily needs and the needs of others, ask His forgiveness for our wrongs, request protection from the evil one, and end on the same note we started— praise. When we pray the way Jesus instructed, according to His will, our prayers are like cruise missiles, always hitting their intended target.

Solomon wrote that hope deferred makes the heart sick, but a longing or prayer fulfilled is a tree of life. Even when we get a "no" or a "not yet" from our Father, He changes our hearts in the most loving way, gently steering us toward the answer He had in mind all along.

> *[The LORD says,] "It shall come to pass that before they call, I will answer; and while they are still speaking, I will hear."*
>
> ISAIAH 65:24 NKJV

The Brass Ring

"I am sure that there is something in Christ's gospel that would soothe and sustain me amid these varied trials if I only knew what it is and how to put forth my hand and take it."

During the heyday of the carousel, riders on the outside row of horses—the stationary ones—were often given a little challenge to grab at the rings dispensed from the carousel. Each time they went around, their excitement built as they stretched out their arms and reached for the ring. Most rings were iron, but one or two per ride were made of brass; if a rider managed to grab a brass ring, it could be redeemed for a free ride. The phrase "going for the brass ring" came to represent striving for the highest prize or living life to the fullest.

In a spiritual sense, those of us who belong to Christ are encouraged to "go for the brass ring" every day of our lives. Reaching out our hands, we press forward to seize what He has called us to do—and to do it with all our might.

The apostle Paul wrote of this *carpe diem* type of zeal in his letter to the believers at Philippi. After stating adamantly that he had not yet reached his goal—or come to the place of completion in Christ—he did do one thing with fervor: forget everything in the past—all the wasted years before he met

Jesus—and reach forward to whatever God had for him in the months and years ahead.

Our own stories may have long, negative subplots that defined who we were before we met Jesus, and if we allow them to, those histories will weigh us down and hinder our growth in God today. That's why it's so important to close the book on that part of our lives and allow the Holy Spirit to write new chapters in our stories.

Does this mean everything is all sweetness and light going forward? No. Does this mean we'll never have another down day? Absolutely not. What it does mean is that *now* we'll have the Son of God holding our hands, leading us each step of the way—giving purpose and meaning to every moment.

Paul was determined to make all his moments count going forward. That's the creed he lived by. Should we who profess faith in Christ do any less?

Forgetting what is behind and straining toward what is ahead,
I press on toward the goal to win the prize for which
God has called me heavenward in Christ Jesus.

PHILIPPIANS 3:13–14

In the Closet

"I have had time to carry my tired, oppressed heart to my compassionate Savior and to tell Him what I cannot utter to any human ear. How strange it is that when, through many years of leisure and strength, prayer was only a task, it is now my chief solace if I can only snatch time for it."

Jesus made it simple. Speaking to a crowd gathered on a hillside, in what has come to be called the Sermon on the Mount, the Rabbi from Nazareth talked to the people in relatable language, getting real with them. His listeners were enthralled. Could it be that God was more than the stern thunder on the mountain their forefathers had known?

Jesus painted a picture of a loving Father who yearned to spend time with His sons and daughters, individually, every chance they took to close themselves in with Him. He also taught them how to pray. First, He let them know that their heavenly Father wasn't impressed by fancy words and long-winded speeches. The Pharisees already had that covered. Instead, He urged them to speak from the heart, one-on-one in a quiet place. Isn't that where we would prefer to have conversations with someone we love deeply? Wouldn't we want that person to speak only to us rather than shouting so that everyone in the area could hear?

It's easy to imagine the Jewish crowd hanging on His every word. They were amazed to learn that God could actually be approached like a friend, like a father. Jesus was turning everything they had ever learned about God on its ear. They knew the shepherd king David spoke of the Lord as if He were a personal friend, but surely Yahweh was austere and unapproachable.

Maybe all we've known of God in the past was that He was a fierce ruler who had prepared a lake of fire for those who might choose not to worship Him. But Jesus came to give us a whole new concept of God. His actions on our behalf made us right with God and gave us access to His throne. Though we had once been enemies, we were now called friends.

When we relax and come to Him simply and humbly, we are sure to find that alone space with God is a place of sweet solace and the most pleasing of rendezvous.

You, O Lord, are good and forgiving,
abounding in steadfast love to all who call on you.

PSALM 86:5 NRSV

Is God Far Away?

"'Christians do not need amusement; they find rest, refreshment, all they want in God.' 'Do you, Father?' 'Alas, no. He seems a great way off.' 'To me He seems very near. So near that He can see every thought of my heart. Dear Father, it is your disease that makes everything so unreal to you. God is really so near, really loves us so, is so sorry for us! And it seems hard, when you are so good and so intent on pleasing Him, that you get no comfort out of Him.'"

Some Christians seem to glide along on an updraft of divine communion, like an eagle soaring without flapping its wings. Others experience those dry-spell seasons when the heavens appear to be made of brass, and God seems to be too busy helping other people or He finally got tired of our whining.

If we're honest, most of us probably fall into the latter category. This experience is particularly hard to take when we are living right before God and not harboring secret sins. We pray, but God seems far away—distant and silent. We start to wonder, does He even care?

Thumbing through the Psalms, we see that another God-seeker felt the same way. His name was David, and he penned most of this poetry-laden book. In Psalm 13, four times David cries, "How long?" to God. At this point in his life, David didn't just need some comfort for loneliness or a reassuring promise about his future. His very life was at stake. His enemy was hot on his heels, seeking to kill him.

Psalm 13 tells us what to do when God seems distant. The psalm is broken into three stanzas of two verses each: the problem (vv. 1–2), the petition (vv. 3–4), and the praise (vv. 5–6). The first stanza is a visceral cry from the heart, the second is a more subdued petition for God's intervention, and the third is a gentle but joyful assertion of praise that God will come through.

After his loud rant, David begins to reason with God in the second stanza, reminding him of what may happen if He doesn't intervene. Finally, in the third stanza, he bolsters his own soul with declarations of praise. Are David's problems suddenly over? No, but now his heart and his head are in alignment with God's—and that's when miracles can happen.

> *How long, LORD? Will you forget me forever? . . . But I trust*
> *in your unfailing love; my heart rejoices in your salvation.*
> *I will sing the LORD's praise, for he has been good to me.*
>
> PSALM 13:1, 5–6

The Singing Heart

"'Well, God is good at any rate, and He would never have sent His Son to die for you if He did not love you.' So then I began to sing. Father likes to hear me sing, and the sweet sense I had that all I had been saying was true and more than true made me sing with joyful heart. I hope it is not a mere miserable presumption that makes me dare to talk so to poor Father. Of course he is ten times better than I am and knows ten times as much, but his disease, whatever it is, keeps his mind befogged. I mean to begin now to pray that light may shine into his soul. It would be delightful to see the peace of God shining in that pale, stern face!"

In the movie *The Sound of Music*, a young nun who feels like a black sheep among her white-woolen sisters at the convent escapes to the high slopes of the Austrian Alps of Salzburg to sing her heart out—to God, to the sky, to anyone who will listen.

There, alone on the sloping meadows, she sings, "The hills are alive with the sound of music!" Always hearing a melody in her natural surroundings—the birdsong, the tinkle of a mountain stream—she opens her mouth to give voice to all the longing and frustration and wonder she's feeling inside.

And something wonderful happens. Music makes a way for a new life to open up before her. When that indefinable longing of her heart gets expressed verbally, the pieces of the puzzle begin to fall into place.

No, we don't literally sing our way to getting what we want, but a peculiar dynamic is at work when our hearts and our words finally synchronize with the unspoken desires we've locked inside.

The real story of Maria von Trapp mirrored the movie version only in part, but one thing about it remains true: what started as a simple act of service led to a journey of self-discovery and a life-altering decision to plunge into God's destiny for her life.

A joyful heart is a heart in tune with the Creator's harmonies, following His lead and reverberating with all the chords of His grace. When we, like Maria, give voice to our longings, we may be pleasantly surprised at the result, too.

> *How good it is to sing praises to our God; for he is gracious, and a song of praise is fitting. . . . Sing to the LORD with thanksgiving; make melody to our God on the lyre.*

PSALM 147:1, 7 NRSV

Voyage's End

"'It is true that I expressed no anxiety when I believed death to be at hand. I felt none. I had given myself away to Christ and He had received me, and why should I be afraid to take His hand and go where He led me? And it is true that I asked for no counsel. I was too weak to ask questions or to like to have questions asked; but my mind was bright and wide awake while my body was so feeble, and I took counsel of God.'"

The apostle Paul expressed genuine ambivalence over his impending death as he wrote to Timothy from his cell in Rome. "The time of my departure is at hand" (2 Timothy 4:6 NKJV), he wrote, realistic yet hopeful to the last.

In a letter to the believers in Rome he struggled to decide which was better: to stay alive and keep training them up in the faith, or to die—to go and be with the Lord he loved. Paul and other first-century Christians actually saw the death of a believer as a blessed event. Of course they grieved; they missed their loved ones as much as we do. Yet they knew their friend or family member was truly with the Lord.

One author describes their mindset toward death and the afterlife not as a towering brick wall beyond which we cannot reach but rather a low stone wall that runs between these two realities: our earthly mortal life on one side and our heavenly immortal life on the other. The veil that runs between—or low stone wall—is so thin we can glance over and rejoice with our loved ones' new existence.

If we're honest with ourselves, many of us wrestle with death and dying. We see it in our reluctance to say the words, calling it "passed away" or "passed on" as a gentler euphemism. We think if we don't actually say *he died* or *she died*, the reality won't strike as hard. But death's reality cannot be avoided—not by anyone. It is the ultimate act of faith when we close our eyes and trust our mortal selves to the One we cannot see. The better we have come to know Him in life, the easier that last step will be.

Faith is the confidence that what we hope for will actually happen;
it gives us assurance about things we cannot see.

HEBREWS 11:1 NLT

Heavy Is the Crown

"Next to being a perfect wife, I want to be a perfect mother. How mortifying, how dreadful in all things to come short of even one's own standard! What approach, then, does one make to God's standard?"

The saying "heavy is the head that wears the crown" usually applies to leadership or politics, but in reality we form crowns of our own making for roles as commonplace as wife and mother.

Whether we grew up with June Cleaver for a mother or Mommy Dearest, we know that every woman who is given the gift of motherhood sets high standards and starts out with a perfect scorecard. And then reality sets in—her little sweetheart throws a tantrum in public, her teenager curses her a blue streak, her adult children are too busy to stay in touch—and she wonders where she went wrong. The problem is perception.

Though we tend to put them on a pedestal, wives and mothers are just women, regular human beings. Having a child may bring out traits of gentleness, patience, and fortitude, but it does not make them instant saints. Fortunately, God understands that—even better than we do—and He promises to work with both mothers and fathers to give their children what they need. He asks that, with His help, mothers and fathers love their children and train them in the fear and admonition of the Lord. Then He gives this assurance: If as parents, you do those two things, no matter how many times you mess up, you'll be able to lay your heads on your pillows at night with peace in your hearts.

The legacy of a godly mother is a blessing that spans generations, and her godliness will be remembered more than her failings. In the Old Testament, we read about Hannah, the mother of the prophet Samuel. She delivered her son to the high priest to be raised in the temple as she had vowed to God she would do. We can hardly comprehend the degree of sacrificial love this must have required. The apostle Paul praised Timothy's mother, Eunice, and his grandmother, Lois, who had guided him to a sincere faith and prepared him for ministry.

Instead of fashioning a weighty crown for her head, we should encourage the mothers we know to simply do the "two things" God requires—and leave the results to Him.

Train children in the right way,
and when old, they will not stray.

PROVERBS 22:6 NRSV

Standing Still

"One by one I am giving up the sweetest maternal duties. God means that I shall be nothing and do nothing, a mere useless sufferer. But when I tell Ernest so, he says I am everything to him and that God's children please Him just as well when they sit patiently with folded hands, if that is His will, as when they are hard at work. But to be at work, to be useful, to be necessary to my husband and children is just what I want; and I do find it hard to be set against the wall, as it were, like an old piece of furniture no longer of any service. I see now that my first desire has not been to please God but to please myself, for I am restless under His restraining hand and find my prison a very narrow one. I would be willing to bear any other trial if I could only have health and strength for my beloved ones. I pray for patience with bitter tears."

Sometimes, standing still is the hardest thing to do in the Christian life. Everything within us wants to fight back in our own strength or try to fix things that God is taking too long to address. Walking in faith sounds good—it has the ring of purpose and vigorous intent about it. And sitting? Well, okay, we can *be seated* with Christ in all His glory and power. But stand still? The very notion sounds like inactivity and purposelessness.

But standing still often takes the greatest discipline and

tests our spiritual mettle. Do we still believe we can fight the good fight of faith on our own, or are we ready to let Christ live our lives through us?

The Bible says a great deal about spiritual warfare, clothing ourselves in God's armor, being strong and courageous. But it would seem that we are not fit for battle until we have learned to stand still. God wants us to be prepared before we go out into the fight. That preparation includes times of calculated waiting. As long as we are straining to go forward, we are not ready for war. But once we have learned to stand still with our ears ready to hear our Master's command, we are equipped to be of great service to Him.

> *The Lord direct your hearts into the love of God,*
> *and into the patient waiting for Christ.*

2 THESSALONIANS 3:5 KJV

Mountain Climbing

"The way of salvation is to me a wide path, absolutely radiant with the glory of Him who shines upon it. I see my shortcomings; I see my sins; but I feel myself bathed, as it were, in the effulgent glow that proceeds directly from the throne of God and the Lamb. It seems as if I ought to have some misgivings about my salvation, but I can hardly say that I have one. How strange, how mysterious that is!"

The group of high schoolers had gathered at the summer camp perched high in the Smoky Mountains for one reason: fun! News traveled fast among the students about this one golden week each summer when Mr. P rented a bus, headed northbound on I-75, and delivered twenty select sophomores to a remote encampment. The precise events of the week were kept under wraps, but one detail always leaked out: the ten-mile, overnight hike up a mountain—and back again.

Every year, the stories trickled back about what happened "on the mountain." Invariably, somebody threw up, another person got poison ivy, someone nearly plummeted into a ravine, and the group of guys and girls bonded around a campfire talking about life and God. The camping trip was unforgettable.

On the ride home, one girl made a keen observation: when they first started up the mountain, the backpack she was forced to carry seemed impossibly heavy. She was sure she'd never make it all those miles with twenty pounds of gear on her back—but she did. About halfway up the mountain, something curious happened. Caught up in the beauty of the woods and the chatter of her fellow hikers, she almost forgot about the weight on her back.

As hike leader, Mr. P passed instructions back to the hikers along the trail, reassuring them of how well they were doing. By the time they reached the mountaintop, the girl had found her rhythm and the backpack, strangely, seemed a part of her. If pressed to remember the early steps of the hike, she found herself unable to recall details—and rushed to tell anyone who would listen about how wonderful the view was from the mountaintop instead.

Our Christian sojourn is much like a long, steady climb up a mountain, but if we don't fall back, one day we, too, will reach the summit. What will our memory of the trek be: a trudging plod or a joyful journey with our Savior?

> *[Be] strengthened with all power according to his glorious might so that you may have great endurance and patience.*

> COLOSSIANS 1:11

Schooled in Sorrow

*"'I have been sick, and I know what sorrow means,' I said.
'And I am glad that I do. For I have learned Christ in that school,
and I know that He can comfort when no one else can.'"*

God whispers to us in our pleasures, speaks to us in our conscience, but shouts in our pains: It is His megaphone to rouse a deaf world," wrote C. S. Lewis.

When everything in life is going along to our pleasing, with success and blessings on all sides, we are prone to "forget" God and therefore have no need of Him. After all, we're good! Life couldn't be better.

But the moment calamity strikes or tragedy springs on us or hardship weighs us down, we rush to our knees crying out, "Lord, how could You let this happen? Please do something!" A sad but true commentary about our fickle human nature.

Throughout the story of God's intervention in human history, we see this pattern repeated again and again. All is well and people get lazy; lazy turns into sloppy faith, and sloppy faith turns into a compromised commitment and, eventually, outright backsliding.

The first-century church, so full of zeal and passion for Christ, faced relentless opposition and persecution—to the point that most of its founders died martyrs' deaths. Yet that very suffering became a springboard for radical growth of the Christian faith. The fact that people were willing to die for Jesus seemed to draw, rather than repel, new converts to the cause.

Anytime God wants to take us to the next level in our spiritual maturity, He turns up the heat. He applies pressure where before we had ease. He makes us uncomfortable so that we are forced to run to Him for help, for answers, for relief. And as we talk with Him, we grow closer to our Father and stronger in the faith. Suddenly, we sense the Holy Spirit as an ever-present companion—one we had perhaps pushed aside for a while.

God allows this because He knows what we were created to be, to do, to achieve. Those goals won't be met as long as we are careless and complacent. But on that cutting edge of faith—well, that's where miracles happen, and we become the army of God.

Sickness, sorrow, hardship—our God doesn't inflict us with trouble, but He does use every circumstance in our lives to grow us up and cause us to rely on Him.

For Christ's sake, I delight in weaknesses, in insults, in hardships, in persecutions, in difficulties. For when I am weak, then I am strong.

2 CORINTHIANS 12:10

Living Stones

"Every day brings its own duty and its own discipline. How is it that I make such slow progress while this is the case? It is a marvel to me why God allows characters like mine to defile His Church. I can only account for it with the thought that if I ever am perfected, I shall be a great honor to His name, for surely worse material for building up a temple of the Holy Ghost was never gathered together before. The time may come when those who know me now, crude, childish, incomplete, will look upon me with amazement, saying, 'What hath God wrought!'"

A contractor building a house starts out with materials in the rough—wood, brick, stone, concrete block—and constructs a thing of beauty and usefulness. From the coarse substance of his raw materials emerges a design of his own making, a vision of a house he saw in his mind long before he set the first brick in place and sealed it with mortar.

The apostle Peter called believers "living stones" who make up the spiritual house of God, with Jesus as the chief cornerstone. As architect and contractor, Jesus had this divine house in mind long before we were even born, and He knew the part each of us would play. Some of us start out as splintery chunks of wood. But over the years our Builder shapes us and sands us down, carving ornamental beauty into what used to be a plain old chunk of wood.

Others of us are made into bricks and then set in place by the Master's trowel. He has just the right place for us, even when we think we'd prefer to be set somewhere else in the house. Unlike other materials, we actually grow more beautiful with age—mellowed and subdued.

Still others of us are stone or concrete block, and we feel our own strength and heft apart from the Builder's touch. When we realize He intends a very special purpose for us, we are happy to line the walls of the house.

Over time, as the house is built, we are transformed into something the Builder imagined all along: functional and lovely. Living stones making up a vibrant spiritual habitation for God. And those who knew us before our Builder molded and used us for His glory may look at the change in us, too, and say, "What hath God wrought!"

Christ Jesus himself [is] the chief cornerstone. In him the whole building is joined together and rises to become a holy temple in the Lord.

Ephesians 2:20–21

Reasons to Rejoice

"I have everything to inspire me to devotion. My dear mother's influence is always upon me. To her I owe the habit of flying to God in every emergency and of believing in prayer. Then I am in close fellowship with a true man and a true Christian. . . . How he has helped me on! God bless him for it! Then I have James. To be with him one half hour is an inspiration. He lives in such blessed communion with Christ that he is in perpetual sunshine, and his happiness fertilizes even this disordered household. . . . And there are my children! My darling, precious children! For their sakes I am continually constrained to seek after an amended, a sanctified life; what I want them to become I must become myself. So I enter on a new year, not knowing what it will bring forth, but surely with a thousand reasons for thanksgiving, for joy, and for hope."

Flanked by other believers and filled with the Holy Spirit, we have limitless reasons to rejoice, starting each new day—and each new year—with praises to God on our lips. But how do we get to this place of perpetual praise, regardless of our circumstances?

Corrie ten Boom, a courageous Dutch woman, became a victim of Nazi oppression when she and her family harbored Jews during the dark days of the Holocaust. She and her sister Betsie were sent to Ravensbruck, a Nazi concentration camp.

When she emerged years later, the sole survivor of her family, she put her experience down on paper.

Corrie was bothered by the fleas that were uncontrolled in their barracks. Hearing her grumbling, her sister Betsie encouraged her to thank God for everything, even the fleas. Corrie grudgingly muttered a prayer of thanks for the fleas. Over the next several months, the sisters realized that the prison guards were bypassing their area. As a result, the women in their barracks were not being assaulted by the guards, and the ten Boom sisters were able to hold Bible studies and prayer meetings. Years later, Corrie learned that the fleas were responsible for keeping the guards away.

The psalmist David commanded his mouth to sing praises to God even when he was fleeing for his life from a powerful enemy. Praising, therefore, springs from our hearts—and out of our mouths—by a decision of our will.

Let his faithful people rejoice in this honor and sing for joy on their beds. May the praise of God be in their mouths.

PSALM 149:5–6

Skimming Off the Dross

"I have been much impressed by Dr. Cabot's sermons today.
While I am listening to his voice and hear him speak of the beauty
and desirableness of the Christian life, I feel as he feels that I am
willing to count all things but dross that I may win Christ. But when
I come home to my worldly cares, I get completely absorbed in them;
and it is only by a painful wrench that I force my soul back to God."

Silver is considered a precious metal, but this costly metal undergoes a rigorous process of purifying before it becomes the stuff of which jewelry and countless ornamental adornments are made. During the refining process of silver ore and scrap silver, the pure silver is separated from the dross—the scum that forms on the surface of molten metal—when it's heated to 1,200 degrees Celsius in a special furnace. Interestingly, the heat releases poisonous chlorine gas as it produces the pure silver.

Another method of refining silver, called the Patio Process, was used in Latin America by the Spaniards during the sixteenth century. First the silversmith ground silver ore to a powder and mixed it with salt, powdered roast copper, and liquid mercury. He then poured the powdered mixture onto a small circle of earth and repeatedly drove a mule team over it until the pressure of their feet crushed the powder into even smaller granules. When the mixture dissolved in the liquid mercury, it was distilled like liquor and then placed in a special furnace. The refined silver that emerged from the furnace was pure.

God works in our lives much like a divine silversmith, choosing His purification method carefully and making sure the process custom fits each of us. Some people may just need heat to burn off the dross whereas others need the formula of pressure + time + heat before they are purified. Still others may require a zap of Holy Spirit fire, similar to what Saul of Tarsus experienced as he traveled the road to Damascus to murder Christians—having no clue he was literally about to be blinded by the Light.

Sanctification—the lifetime process of honing, shaping, sanding, molding, and purifying that each of us believers undergoes—is what marks us as true Christians. As Jesus said, we are identified by our fruits, or what we say and do. Because when He turns up the heat, all but true disciples get out of the kitchen.

You were washed, you were sanctified, you were justified in the name of the Lord Jesus Christ and by the Spirit of our God.

1 Corinthians 6:11

Taming Our Tempers

"For me to live in Christ seems natural enough, for I have been driven to Him not only by sorrow but also by sin. Every outbreak of my hasty temper sends me weeping and penitent to the foot of the cross, and I love much because I have been forgiven much."

Jesus called two of His favorite disciples the "Sons of Thunder." They earned that nickname not because they liked to study stormy weather patterns but because they each had a fiery temperament. Yet these boisterous brothers, James and John, would become so transformed by the Son of God that they trained new believers in the first churches and wrote letters that are now part of scripture.

Three years with Jesus set off a character makeover that changed the course of their lives, and time spent with the Savior will do the same for us. Jesus first encountered these hotheaded brothers by the seashore, fishing with their father. Sometime after they left their nets to follow Him, they argued about who would be greatest in the kingdom of heaven. They also wanted to call down fire on a Samaritan town, but Jesus rebuked them.

God has a purpose for everything He does, and He chose these men because He saw what was inside them—the potential hidden within waiting to be unleashed by the Holy Spirit. That same fiery nature that served to make the brothers loud and overbearing would also fuel a passion for souls someday, so much so that James became the first apostle to give his life for the cause of Christ.

That day by the shore of Galilee when they left their nets, these coarse fishermen never dreamed that the Man who called them—the very Son of God—would turn their lives upside down, and then someday use *them* to turn the world upside down for Him.

God knows our hearts, and He sees just what is inside of us: the good, the bad, and the ugly. He isn't surprised by what He finds there, and He doesn't find it daunting. In other words, we can relax. He really knows us, and He loves us anyway. But He does want to do His restoration work inside us. If we say yes He will weed out the bad, and the ugly, and transform the good into the godly.

> *"I will give them singleness of heart and put a new spirit within them. I will take away their stony, stubborn heart and give them a tender, responsive heart."*

> EZEKIEL 11:19 NLT

A Glorious Passage

> *"We must not forget that God is honored or dishonored by the way a Christian dies as well as by the way in which he lives. There is great significance in the description given in the Bible of the death by which John should "Glorify God" (John 21:19); to my mind it implies that to die well is to live well."*

Everyone always said she was the black sheep of the family, the tomboyish middle daughter who struggled to figure out where she fit among her four sisters, where she fit in the work world, even where she fit in the church. Growing up with taunts hurled at her back, she learned to slouch when she walked and hide her emotions under a scowl every time a family snapshot was taken. While each of her sisters got married and had children, no one came for her. Love, like God, seemed to have passed her by.

But something wonderful happened in the midpoint of her life: she met Jesus. Suddenly this rough-mouthed woman with no friends discovered her purpose in life, and she embraced it with zeal.

Her assignment was to teach Sunday school. Few could figure out what drew the kids to this formerly dour-faced woman. Maybe it was her smile or her blunt way of speaking.

Or maybe it was the way she could slug a baseball out on the church's sandlot.

Years went by and the woman got old. But her former students in Sunday school remembered her and kept tabs as they grew up, got married, and had children of their own.

One day she called her youngest sister and said she knew she wasn't long for this world. Soon it would be time to "go home," as she put it. She could no longer take care of herself. On the evening of her first day in the nursing home, she talked to her sister by phone and then said good night. The next morning a call came from the nursing home staff: "Your sister died last night," a nurse said.

The younger sister rushed to the nursing home and lifted the blanket covering her sister's face. On it was that permanent grin, as if she'd only hopped over a fence to play with those waiting on the other side.

Truly, how we die speaks volumes about how we lived. Will ours be a terror-filled crossing—the death of the unbelieving— or a glorious passage as we go home to our Father?

> *Those who walk uprightly enter into peace;*
> *they find rest as they lie in death.*

ISAIAH 57:2

A Bittersweet Longing

"As I listen, I realize that it is to [Mother] I owe that early, deep-seated longing to please the Lord Jesus, which I never remember as having a beginning or an ending, though it did have its fluctuations."

Why is it that sunsets are more bittersweet—and hence more wonderful—than sunrises? Professor C. S. Lewis asks his class in the movie *Shadowlands*. Why does God give us so many wonderful things in this world, yet leave us hungry for more? Why are we never quite able to fill that hole in our hearts that aches with a longing we can't put into words?

If there's one thing we can count on, it's that God refuses to stay in the religion boxes we fashion for Him. Once we think we have Him figured out, He upsets all our carefully wrought plans and turns left when we were sure He'd take a right.

We see Him working in our lives and rejoice, thinking, *Yes, this is the expected course I wished for.* But no sooner do we set out with our rehearsed lines than He flips the script—planting us into scenes and plot twists we couldn't have imagined. Yet His ways are wondrous and beyond our comprehension.

Lewis was a middle-aged bachelor, content with his teaching life at Magdalen College in Oxford, England. Leading a quiet, scholarly life, he filled his days with lecturing and reading and lively pub debates with his professorial friends, who called themselves The Inklings. And then into his quietly ordered life came a woman—a divorced *American* woman at that—upsetting his apple cart and overturning everything he called normal.

C. S. Lewis never counted on finding the love of a woman, but God sent her anyway. And because of a friendship that blossomed into love, the world is gifted with some of Lewis's most profound writing.

We, too, may find the romantic love of our lives, or be blessed with the love of children or good friends, but nothing—absolutely nothing—can fill that deep longing in our souls placed there by God. Is it any wonder that human relationships always disappoint us in some way, never quite attaining (or sustaining) the fullness we'd hoped for? The One who created us has made it so that only He can fill that deep soul-longing in our hearts.

The LORD will vindicate me; your love, LORD, endures forever—
do not abandon the works of your hands.

PSALM 138:8

The Cost of Motherhood

"What a fearful thing it is to be a mother! But I have given my child to God. I would not recall him if I could. I am thankful He has counted me worthy to present Him so costly a gift. . . . Above all let me remember God's lovingkindness and tender mercy. He has not left us to the bitterness of a grief that refuses and disdains to be comforted. We believe in Him, we love Him, we worship Him as we never did before."

Susanna Wesley is known as the mother of Methodism primarily because two of her sons, John Wesley and Charles Wesley, proved her mettle through their teaching and godly living. Although she never wrote a book or preached a sermon, it's a title she legitimately earned.

Life in seventeenth-century England on a clergyman's salary was hard and made even harder because Susanna and Samuel Wesley had nineteen children. Nine of her children died as infants. Four of the children who died were twins. A maid accidentally smothered one child. At her death, only eight of Susanna's children were still alive.

At one point her husband abandoned the family for over a year after a minor dispute, but Susanna managed to keep them all together and find time to make each child feel loved. When she needed time alone with God, she would sit with her apron over her head in a makeshift "prayer closet." Her life was one of almost continual hardship, yet history remembers her as the woman who molded two of the church's most influential leaders.

It is a fearful thing indeed to be entrusted with the care and rearing of children, and all the more so when we are committed to passing the baton of Christianity to the next generation. What we say to our children matters immensely, but what we *do* matters even more—for they are constantly watching our example.

While we may not be called upon to endure our own child's death, hardship and suffering may accompany our motherhood in other ways—a backslidden adult child, a son or daughter whose own children face illness or death, a child who resents our influence in his or her life and cuts off all contact. But if we remain faithful to love these souls that are on loan to us from God for a little while, joy will surely come, whether in this life or the next.

Do not forsake your mother's teaching. Bind them always on your heart; fasten them around your neck. When you walk, they will guide you.

PROVERBS 6:20–22

Living and Loving

"My dear Ernest has felt this sorrow to his heart's core. But he has not for one moment questioned the goodness or the love of our Father in thus taking from us the child who promised to be our greatest earthly joy. Our consent to God's will has drawn us together very closely; together we bear the yoke in our youth, together we pray and sing praises in the very midst of our tears. 'I was dumb, I opened not my mouth; because thou didst it' (Psalm 39:9)."

To live is to experience great heights and deep valleys, to know love and pain in equal measure, yet still—if given the chance to decide—most of us would choose life, especially when we are committed to Christ.

In the great stories of faith that are passed down through the generations, a common thread emerges: God rescues us from mediocrity and meaningless existence, fills us with Himself, implants purpose and destiny in our lives, and then suffering comes. Peter, the bold disciple upon whom Jesus built His church, said that God was watching and that after our brief time of suffering was complete, He would be faithful to heal and restore.

Pop-culture Christianity often dispenses a kind of fluff Gospel, promising seekers that a life of nonstop blessing and favor and goodness awaits them if they will just sign on the dotted line. But Jesus Himself, and certainly His first followers, warned and *experienced* otherwise, knowing that true discipleship always comes at a high cost. Most of them paid with their lives.

Tragedy and hardship expose what is in our hearts, and the test of our character may sometimes prove too much. Some couples are torn apart from the death of a child, yet another couple who faces the same tragedy is strangely drawn closer together—and closer to their God. Before they faced tragedy, we might not have been able to tell which pair would fall apart and which would fall together.

In the midst of our pain and suffering, God wraps His arms around us and gently leads us onward, sometimes into areas we never thought we might tread. But the day will come when our tears are turned into rejoicing, and night gives way to morning.

The God of all grace, who called you to his eternal glory in Christ, after you have suffered a little while, will himself restore you and make you strong, firm and steadfast.

1 PETER 5:10

Reason Unknown

"My comfort is in my perfect faith in the goodness and love of my Father, my certainty that He had a reason in thus afflicting me that I should admire and adore if I knew what it was. And in the midst of my sorrow I have had and do have a delight in Him hitherto unknown, so that sometimes this room in which I am a prisoner seems like the very gate of heaven."

$\mathcal{S}$uffering and sorrow may be wielded in God's hand as tools to refine us, but sometimes hardships come simply because God wants to test us—to see how much, or how little, we love Him.

Job's tale is so widely known that even people unfamiliar with the Bible equate his name with suffering unduly, and the story itself can be mistaken for fable. But it really happened, and God made a faithful record of Job's story so that later generations could learn from it.

Described as a good man who pleased God, Job lived a life of wealth and blessing and divine favor. So when the devil accused Job before God, claiming he was only righteous because he was so blessed, God allowed the devil to test him.

This good and godly man suffered horribly at Satan's hand, losing his wealth, his health, and his family. Like Job's so-called friends, we always equate suffering with guilt. "He must have done something," we reason. "What did she do to deserve

God's punishment?" we whisper behind our hands. Or even: *Why is God so angry with me?*

But Job teaches us that we can't assume God is displeased and that we must *do something* to earn His favor again. We sometimes think that if we can "make good," God will ease our sorrow, end our suffering, and all will be well again. We beg Him for answers, waiting to hear so we can fix things.

But God often sends trials and tests in a box marked REASON UNKNOWN. The boxes come in different shapes and sizes—some gift-wrapped and others unadorned. Regardless, we are helpless to refuse them. It is how we *receive* them that makes all the difference.

Will we curse God and blunder on, or say with Job, "The LORD gave, and the LORD has taken away; blessed be the name of the LORD" (Job 1:21 NKJV)?

> *Rejoice in hope, be patient*
> *in suffering, persevere in prayer.*
>
> ROMANS 12:12 NRSV

Soul Under Construction

"During my long illness and confinement to my room, the Bible has been almost a new book to me; and I see that God has always dealt with His children as He deals with them now and that no new thing has befallen me. All these weary days so full of languor, these nights so full of unrest have had their appointed mission to my soul. And perhaps I have had no discipline so salutary as this forced inaction and uselessness at a time when youth and natural energy continually cried out for room and work."

When we are born again, the Holy Spirit tacks a sign up on our foreheads that reads SOUL UNDER CONSTRUCTION, and so begins our long spiritual refurbishment program. Sometimes He takes the path we least expected—not one littered with hurdles and potholes, but a quieter road of "forced inaction and uselessness" at a time when we expected Him to launch us into our grand destiny.

Four walls can become God's classroom for Spiritual Growth 101, with the Bible as our only textbook and the Holy Spirit our Teacher. We thought He was ready to send us out on a mission field, whether overseas or in our workplace, but instead we find that *we* are the mission field and God performs His quiet, steady work on *us*. And oftentimes entire destinies are created out of quiet time spent within the closeness of a room.

Such was the case for English poet Elizabeth Barrett Browning. An invalid with a vivid talent, she spent most of her adult life within the space of her bedroom, writing poems and sonnets that caught the ear of the literary world. Through a family friend and patron of the arts, Elizabeth met the man who would become her husband—Robert Browning—and the two heavily influenced each other's writing. Because of her love story with Robert, Elizabeth generated her most famous sonnet, "How Do I Love Thee?" (Sonnet 43).

Much of Elizabeth Barrett Browning's work carries a religious theme. She believed that the Christian faith was essentially poetry glorified. After struggling with declining health for so long, Elizabeth died in her husband's arms. He said that she died smiling.

God may be up to something surprising in our own life stories, dropping purpose and meaning into even our long drought seasons and quiet hours. And just when we think destiny has passed us by, we may be on the verge of breaking forth into our true calling.

It is God who works in you to will and to act in order to fulfill his good purpose.

PHILIPPIANS 2:13

"I Will Show You"

"We are at peace with each other and at peace with God;
His dealings with us do not perplex or puzzle us,
though we do not pretend to understand them."

A man who lived thousands of years ago found favor with God in the midst of a pagan culture that worshipped idols. What exactly set this man apart we do not know, but God saw something in his heart—especially his belief that the voice he heard whispering in his spirit was the voice of the one true God.

So strong was this man's faith that when God spoke, Abraham obeyed. "Pack up your family and go to a land that I will show you," the Lord said. And so he did.

Can we imagine a vaguer injunction? Leave all that's familiar to you, all you hold dear, everything you've known in your life thus far—your extended family, your livelihood—and go to the place that I will show you. Not go to this place or that place but "[go]. . .to a land that *I will show you*" (Genesis 12:1 NKJV, emphasis added). Parts unknown except by God.

How many of us would be willing to chuck it all in for the words of a voice in our heads? Yet, to his credit, Abraham sensed that this was the real deal. This Voice, he knew, had the markings of true divinity. Not mute wooden idols fashioned by man's hands but something so big, so real, so powerful that when He spoke it changed everything.

It's a bit of a paradox to say we aren't perplexed by God's dealings with us, and yet we don't pretend that we understand them. But this sentiment describes exactly what Abraham must have felt as he pulled up the stakes of his tent, loaded his camels, and set out for only God knew where.

Turns out God did know exactly what He was doing and caused this man—this one man He'd set apart—to be the father of a nation—Israel—and the father of the faith we call Christianity.

When we hear that same God whisper in our hearts, how do we respond? Do we shush His voice or cover it over with busyness, or do we pull up our stakes and follow Him—wherever He might lead us?

[Abram] believed the LORD; and the
LORD reckoned it to him as righteousness.

GENESIS 15:6 NRSV

Love and Loyalty

"This is the testimony of all the good books, sermons, hymns, and memoirs I read—that God's ways are infinitely perfect; that we are to love Him for what He is and therefore equally as much when He afflicts as when He prospers us; that there is no real happiness but in doing and suffering His will; and that this life is but a scene of probation through which we pass to the real life above."

The words of the traditional wedding vows could double as our personal creed as we follow in the steps of Christ. For just as a man leaves his home to join himself to his wife, Jesus left His home in heaven to wed Himself to us, His spiritual bride. When we say "I do" to Jesus, we are making a very solemn commitment.

No question about it, Christ has already made a commitment to us. His vows are consecrated by His shed blood and broken body. He has the right to ask for all our love and loyalty, because He has already given us His—not only in word but also in deed.

Now here's the amazing part. God knew that as much as we might want to, we human beings are simply unable to keep our vows to Him. So He has given us a Helper, someone to teach us how to make good on our promises to Him. The apostle Paul wrote about this when he says that it is Christ in us—the hope of glory—who lives in and through us and brings us step-by-step along the path of righteousness. We can't do it without Him. If anyone could have succeeded, the ancient Hebrews would have done so, but though they tried to keep every letter of God's commandments, human fallibility always prevailed.

And so Jesus came to bridge the gap, reuniting us with our Father and offering us a divine marriage contract. Our part is simply to say yes; He does all the heavy lifting, including lifting us out of a life of meaninglessness and mundane existence and setting us on a path of adventure that only He could devise.

The only words of the traditional wedding vows that don't apply in our marriage to Jesus are those last few—"from this day forward *till death do us part*"—because death brings us instantly, joyously, into His presence forevermore.

Keep yourselves in God's love as you wait for the mercy
of our Lord Jesus Christ to bring you to eternal life.

JUDE 1:21

Eventide

"Oh, these fluctuations in my religious life amaze me! I cannot doubt that I am really God's child; it would be a dishonor to Him to doubt it. I cannot doubt that I have held as real communion with Him as with any earthly friend—and oh, it has been far sweeter!"

$\mathscr{C}$an we for just one moment fathom how much we mean to our Father God? He didn't have to create us; He wanted to. He longed for companionship with His created beings and looked forward to spending time with us: heart to heart, voice to voice, each of his or her own free will.

Some consider the story of Adam and Eve too far-fetched to be real, and yet everything God laid out in the beginning lines up with the reality of the world as we know it. Every word God speaks is true, and all the promises of God come to pass. His most profound promise is that He would be a Father to us and we could be His sons and daughters, calling Him "Daddy" just as Jesus did. When the Holy Spirit takes up residence in our hearts, we can have one-to-one communication with our Father that's as real as any relationship here on earth.

This broken world still turns, but a day is coming when everything will be made new again—just as it was in the beginning. Sin and suffering will be eradicated and love will

204

be the rule of law. Sickness, pain, and disease will be no more. Crying will cease—for good. There will be no need for courts because there will be no crime. The oceans, rivers, and streams will flow clean and unpolluted. Every person will have enough to eat and drink. Divisions between nations will be abandoned and war will no longer require its sober sacrifices. Love and peace and joy will be the rule of the day, and God's presence will be felt by every man, woman, and child.

Sounds crazy, right? Far-fetched, like some cosmic fairy tale too fantastic to be true. But God has promised. He's given us a written contract to support that promise. It's called the Bible. Finally, there will be a new and better world for all of us. But there is one thing that will not change. If we have walked in communion with God here on this earth, we will walk and talk with Him still—only then face-to-face.

> *In keeping with his promise we are looking forward to a*
> *new heaven and a new earth, where righteousness dwells.*

2 PETER 3:13

Peace Like a River

"Yes, I love everybody! That crowning joy has come to me at last. Christ is in my soul; He is mine. . .and His Spirit flows forth from mine in the calm peace of a river whose banks are green with grass and glad with flowers. If I die, it will be to leave a wearied and worn body and a sinful soul to go joyfully to be with Christ, to weary and to sin no more. If I live, I shall find much blessed work to do for Him. So living or dying, I shall be the Lord's. But I wish, oh, how earnestly, that whether I go or stay, I could inspire some lives with the joy that is now mine. . . . But not till I was shut up to prayer and to study of God's word by the loss of earthly joys, sickness destroying the flavor of them all, did I begin to penetrate the mystery that is learned under the cross. And wondrous as it is, how simple is this mystery! To love Christ and to know that I love Him—this is all!"

Horatio Spafford wrote one of the church's most famous hymns after two major traumas in his life. The first was the Great Chicago Fire of 1871, which threw him into financial ruin. The second was the loss of his four daughters, all of whom were killed when their ship collided with another vessel while crossing the Atlantic with their mother.

Several weeks later, as Spafford's own ship passed near the spot where his daughters died, the Holy Spirit inspired the words that became the hymn "It Is Well with My Soul": "when peace, like a river, attendeth my way."

The hymn speaks of the supernatural peace that floods our souls when we are united with Christ, no matter what grief and pain we may endure on earth. Indeed, it's often *through* grief and pain that God gets our attention and does His finest work in us.

Even before the Garden of Eden, God planned to restore us to Himself in perfect relationship through His Son, Jesus. Satan thought he had outwitted God. He thought he had ruined the Creator's plan to fellowship with us, His created beings, but he was wrong.

That perfect peace Spafford knew in the dark hours of his soul was purchased by God's perfect Son, Jesus Christ, for us. No tragedy, no matter how great, can rob us of that peace.

"You will keep him in perfect peace, whose mind is stayed on You, because he trusts in You."

ISAIAH 26:3 NKJV

Scripture Index

Old Testament

New Testament

Read Thru the Bible in a Year

1-Jan	Gen. 1-2	Matt. 1	Ps. 1
2-Jan	Gen. 3-4	Matt. 2	Ps. 2
3-Jan	Gen. 5-7	Matt. 3	Ps. 3
4-Jan	Gen. 8-10	Matt. 4	Ps. 4
5-Jan	Gen. 11-13	Matt. 5:1-20	Ps. 5
6-Jan	Gen. 14-16	Matt. 5:21-48	Ps. 6
7-Jan	Gen. 17-18	Matt. 6:1-18	Ps. 7
8-Jan	Gen. 19-20	Matt. 6:19-34	Ps. 8
9-Jan	Gen. 21-23	Matt. 7:1-11	Ps. 9:1-8
10-Jan	Gen. 24	Matt. 7:12-29	Ps. 9:9-20
11-Jan	Gen. 25-26	Matt. 8:1-17	Ps. 10:1-11
12-Jan	Gen. 27:1-28:9	Matt. 8:18-34	Ps. 10:12-18
13-Jan	Gen. 28:10-29:35	Matt. 9	Ps. 11
14-Jan	Gen. 30:1-31:21	Matt. 10:1-15	Ps. 12
15-Jan	Gen. 31:22-32:21	Matt. 10:16-36	Ps. 13
16-Jan	Gen. 32:22-34:31	Matt. 10:37-11:6	Ps. 14
17-Jan	Gen. 35-36	Matt. 11:7-24	Ps. 15
18-Jan	Gen. 37-38	Matt. 11:25-30	Ps. 16
19-Jan	Gen. 39-40	Matt. 12:1-29	Ps. 17
20-Jan	Gen. 41	Matt. 12:30-50	Ps. 18:1-15
21-Jan	Gen. 42-43	Matt. 13:1-9	Ps. 18:16-29
22-Jan	Gen. 44-45	Matt. 13:10-23	Ps. 18:30-50
23-Jan	Gen. 46:1-47:26	Matt. 13:24-43	Ps. 19
24-Jan	Gen. 47:27-49:28	Matt. 13:44-58	Ps. 20
25-Jan	Gen. 49:29-Exod. 1:22	Matt. 14	Ps. 21
26-Jan	Exod. 2-3	Matt. 15:1-28	Ps. 22:1-21
27-Jan	Exod. 4:1-5:21	Matt. 15:29-16:12	Ps. 22:22-31
28-Jan	Exod. 5:22-7:24	Matt. 16:13-28	Ps. 23
29-Jan	Exod. 7:25-9:35	Matt. 17:1-9	Ps. 24
30-Jan	Exod. 10-11	Matt. 17:10-27	Ps. 25
31-Jan	Exod. 12	Matt. 18:1-20	Ps. 26
1-Feb	Exod. 13-14	Matt. 18:21-35	Ps. 27
2-Feb	Exod. 15-16	Matt. 19:1-15	Ps. 28
3-Feb	Exod. 17-19	Matt. 19:16-30	Ps. 29
4-Feb	Exod. 20-21	Matt. 20:1-19	Ps. 30
5-Feb	Exod. 22-23	Matt. 20:20-34	Ps. 31:1-8
6-Feb	Exod. 24-25	Matt. 21:1-27	Ps. 31:9-18
7-Feb	Exod 26-27	Matt. 21:28-46	Ps. 31:19-24
8-Feb	Exod. 28	Matt. 22	Ps. 32
9-Feb	Exod. 29	Matt. 23:1-36	Ps. 33:1-12
10-Feb	Exod. 30-31	Matt. 23:37-24:28	Ps. 33:13-22
11-Feb	Exod. 32-33	Matt. 24:29-51	Ps. 34:1-7

12-Feb	Exod. 34:1-35:29	Matt. 25:1-13	Ps. 34:8-22
13-Feb	Exod. 35:30-37:29	Matt. 25:14-30	Ps. 35:1-8
14-Feb	Exod. 38-39	Matt. 25:31-46	Ps. 35:9-17
15-Feb	Exod. 40	Matt. 26:1-35	Ps. 35:18-28
16-Feb	Lev. 1-3	Matt. 26:36-68	Ps. 36:1-6
17-Feb	Lev. 4:1-5:13	Matt. 26:69-27:26	Ps. 36:7-12
18-Feb	Lev. 5:14 -7:21	Matt. 27:27-50	Ps. 37:1-6
19-Feb	Lev. 7:22-8:36	Matt. 27:51-66	Ps. 37:7-26
20-Feb	Lev. 9-10	Matt. 28	Ps. 37:27-40
21-Feb	Lev. 11-12	Mark 1:1-28	Ps. 38
22-Feb	Lev. 13	Mark 1:29-39	Ps. 39
23-Feb	Lev. 14	Mark 1:40-2:12	Ps. 40:1-8
24-Feb	Lev. 15	Mark 2:13-3:35	Ps. 40:9-17
25-Feb	Lev. 16-17	Mark 4:1-20	Ps. 41:1-4
26-Feb	Lev. 18-19	Mark 4:21-41	Ps. 41:5-13
27-Feb	Lev. 20	Mark 5	Ps. 42-43
28-Feb	Lev. 21-22	Mark 6:1-13	Ps. 44
1-Mar	Lev. 23-24	Mark 6:14-29	Ps. 45:1-5
2-Mar	Lev. 25	Mark 6:30-56	Ps. 45:6-12
3-Mar	Lev. 26	Mark 7	Ps. 45:13-17
4-Mar	Lev. 27	Mark 8	Ps. 46
5-Mar	Num. 1-2	Mark 9:1-13	Ps. 47
6-Mar	Num. 3	Mark 9:14-50	Ps. 48:1-8
7-Mar	Num. 4	Mark 10:1-34	Ps. 48:9-14
8-Mar	Num. 5:1-6:21	Mark 10:35-52	Ps. 49:1-9
9-Mar	Num. 6:22-7:47	Mark 11	Ps. 49:10-20
10-Mar	Num. 7:48-8:4	Mark 12:1-27	Ps. 50:1-15
11-Mar	Num. 8:5-9:23	Mark 12:28-44	Ps. 50:16-23
12-Mar	Num. 10-11	Mark 13:1-8	Ps. 51:1-9
13-Mar	Num. 12-13	Mark 13:9-37	Ps. 51:10-19
14-Mar	Num. 14	Mark 14:1-31	Ps. 52
15-Mar	Num. 15	Mark 14:32-72	Ps. 53
16-Mar	Num. 16	Mark 15:1-32	Ps. 54
17-Mar	Num. 17-18	Mark 15:33-47	Ps. 55
18-Mar	Num. 19-20	Mark 16	Ps. 56:1-7
19-Mar	Num. 21:1-22:20	Luke 1:1-25	Ps. 56:8-13
20-Mar	Num. 22:21-23:30	Luke 1:26-56	Ps. 57
21-Mar	Num. 24-25	Luke 1:57-2:20	Ps. 58
22-Mar	Num. 26:1-27:11	Luke 2:21-38	Ps. 59:1-8
23-Mar	Num. 27:12-29:11	Luke 2:39-52	Ps. 59:9-17
24-Mar	Num. 29:12-30:16	Luke 3	Ps. 60:1-5
25-Mar	Num. 31	Luke 4	Ps. 60:6-12

26-Mar	Num. 32-33	Luke 5:1-16	Ps. 61
27-Mar	Num. 34-36	Luke 5:17-32	Ps. 62:1-6
28-Mar	Deut. 1:1-2:25	Luke 5:33-6:11	Ps. 62:7-12
29-Mar	Deut. 2:26-4:14	Luke 6:12-35	Ps. 63:1-5
30-Mar	Deut. 4:15-5:22	Luke 6:36-49	Ps. 63:6-11
31-Mar	Deut. 5:23-7:26	Luke 7:1-17	Ps. 64:1-5
1-Apr	Deut. 8-9	Luke 7:18-35	Ps. 64:6-10
2-Apr	Deut. 10-11	Luke 7:36-8:3	Ps. 65:1-8
3-Apr	Deut. 12-13	Luke 8:4-21	Ps. 65:9-13
4-Apr	Deut. 14:1-16:8	Luke 8:22-39	Ps. 66:1-7
5-Apr	Deut. 16:9-18:22	Luke 8:40-56	Ps. 66:8-15
6-Apr	Deut. 19:1-21:9	Luke 9:1-22	Ps. 66:16-20
7-Apr	Deut. 21:10-23:8	Luke 9:23-42	Ps. 67
8-Apr	Deut. 23:9-25:19	Luke 9:43-62	Ps. 68:1-6
9-Apr	Deut. 26:1-28:14	Luke 10:1-20	Ps. 68:7-14
10-Apr	Deut. 28:15-68	Luke 10:21-37	Ps. 68:15-19
11-Apr	Deut. 29-30	Luke 10:38-11:23	Ps. 68:20-27
12-Apr	Deut. 31:1-32:22	Luke 11:24-36	Ps. 68:28-35
13-Apr	Deut. 32:23-33:29	Luke 11:37-54	Ps. 69:1-9
14-Apr	Deut. 34-Josh. 2	Luke 12:1-15	Ps. 69:10-17
15-Apr	Josh. 3:1-5:12	Luke 12:16-40	Ps. 69:18-28
16-Apr	Josh. 5:13-7:26	Luke 12:41-48	Ps. 69:29-36
17-Apr	Josh. 8-9	Luke 12:49-59	Ps. 70
18-Apr	Josh. 10:1-11:15	Luke 13:1-21	Ps. 71:1-6
19-Apr	Josh. 11:16-13:33	Luke 13:22-35	Ps. 71:7-16
20-Apr	Josh. 14-16	Luke 14:1-15	Ps. 71:17-21
21-Apr	Josh. 17:1-19:16	Luke 14:16-35	Ps. 71:22-24
22-Apr	Josh. 19:17-21:42	Luke 15:1-10	Ps. 72:1-11
23-Apr	Josh. 21:43-22:34	Luke 15:11-32	Ps. 72:12-20
24-Apr	Josh. 23-24	Luke 16:1-18	Ps. 73:1-9
25-Apr	Judg. 1-2	Luke 16:19-17:10	Ps. 73:10-20
26-Apr	Judg. 3-4	Luke 17:11-37	Ps. 73:21-28
27-Apr	Judg. 5:1-6:24	Luke 18:1-17	Ps. 74:1-3
28-Apr	Judg. 6:25-7:25	Luke 18:18-43	Ps. 74:4-11
29-Apr	Judg. 8:1-9:23	Luke 19:1-28	Ps. 74:12-17
30-Apr	Judg. 9:24-10:18	Luke 19:29-48	Ps. 74:18-23
1-May	Judg. 11:1-12:7	Luke 20:1-26	Ps. 75:1-7
2-May	Judg. 12:8-14:20	Luke 20:27-47	Ps. 75:8-10
3-May	Judg. 15-16	Luke 21:1-19	Ps. 76:1-7
4-May	Judg. 17-18	Luke 21:20-22:6	Ps. 76:8-12
5-May	Judg. 19:1-20:23	Luke 22:7-30	Ps. 77:1-11
6-May	Judg. 20:24-21:25	Luke 22:31-54	Ps. 77:12-20

7-May	Ruth 1-2	Luke 22:55-23:25	Ps. 78:1-4
8-May	Ruth 3-4	Luke 23:26-24:12	Ps. 78:5-8
9-May	1 Sam. 1:1-2:21	Luke 24:13-53	Ps. 78:9-16
10-May	1 Sam. 2:22-4:22	John 1:1-28	Ps. 78:17-24
11-May	1 Sam. 5-7	John 1:29-51	Ps. 78:25-33
12-May	1 Sam. 8:1-9:26	John 2	Ps. 78:34-41
13-May	1 Sam. 9:27-11:15	John 3:1-22	Ps. 78:42-55
14-May	1 Sam. 12-13	John 3:23-4:10	Ps. 78:56-66
15-May	1 Sam. 14	John 4:11-38	Ps. 78:67-72
16-May	1 Sam. 15-16	John 4:39-54	Ps. 79:1-7
17-May	1 Sam. 17	John 5:1-24	Ps. 79:8-13
18-May	1 Sam. 18-19	John 5:25-47	Ps. 80:1-7
19-May	1 Sam. 20-21	John 6:1-21	Ps. 80:8-19
20-May	1 Sam. 22-23	John 6:22-42	Ps. 81:1-10
21-May	1 Sam. 24:1-25:31	John 6:43-71	Ps. 81:11-16
22-May	1 Sam. 25:32-27:12	John 7:1-24	Ps. 82
23-May	1 Sam. 28-29	John 7:25-8:11	Ps. 83
24-May	1 Sam. 30-31	John 8:12-47	Ps. 84:1-4
25-May	2 Sam. 1-2	John 8:48-9:12	Ps. 84:5-12
26-May	2 Sam. 3-4	John 9:13-34	Ps. 85:1-7
27-May	2 Sam. 5:1-7:17	John 9:35-10:10	Ps. 85:8-13
28-May	2 Sam. 7:18-10:19	John 10:11-30	Ps. 86:1-10
29-May	2 Sam. 11:1-12:25	John 10;31-11:16	Ps. 86:11-17
30-May	2 Sam. 12:26-13:39	John 11:17-54	Ps. 87
31-May	2 Sam. 14:1-15:12	John 11:55-12:19	Ps. 88:1-9
1-Jun	2 Sam. 15:13-16:23	John 12:20-43	Ps. 88:10-18
2-Jun	2 Sam. 17:1-18:18	John 12:44-13:20	Ps. 89:1-6
3-Jun	2 Sam. 18:19-19:39	John 13:21-38	Ps. 89:7-13
4-Jun	2 Sam. 19:40-21:22	John 14:1-17	Ps. 89:14-18
5-Jun	2 Sam. 22:1-23:7	John 14:18-15:27	Ps. 89:19-29
6-Jun	2 Sam. 23:8-24:25	John 16:1-22	Ps. 89:30-37
7-Jun	1 Kings 1	John 16:23-17:5	Ps. 89:38-52
8-Jun	1 Kings 2	John 17:6-26	Ps. 90:1-12
9-Jun	1 Kings 3-4	John 18:1-27	Ps. 90:13-17
10-Jun	1 Kings 5-6	John 18:28-19:5	Ps. 91:1-10
11-Jun	1 Kings 7	John 19:6-25a	Ps. 91:11-16
12-Jun	1 Kings 8:1-53	John 19:25b-42	Ps. 92:1-9
13-Jun	1 Kings 8:54-10:13	John 20:1-18	Ps. 92:10-15
14-Jun	1 Kings 10:14-11:43	John 20:19-31	Ps. 93
15-Jun	1 Kings 12:1-13:10	John 21	Ps. 94:1-11
16-Jun	1 Kings 13:11-14:31	Acts 1:1-11	Ps. 94:12-23
17-Jun	1 Kings 15:1-16:20	Acts 1:12-26	Ps. 95

18-Jun	1 Kings 16:21-18:19	Acts 2:1-21	Ps. 96:1-8
19-Jun	1 Kings 18:20-19:21	Acts2:22-41	Ps. 96:9-13
20-Jun	1 Kings 20	Acts 2:42-3:26	Ps. 97:1-6
21-Jun	1 Kings 21:1-22:28	Acts 4:1-22	Ps. 97:7-12
22-Jun	1 Kings 22:29- 2 Kings 1:18	Acts 4:23-5:11	Ps. 98
23-Jun	2 Kings 2-3	Acts 5:12-28	Ps. 99
24-Jun	2 Kings 4	Acts 5:29-6:15	Ps. 100
25-Jun	2 Kings 5:1-6:23	Acts 7:1-16	Ps. 101
26-Jun	2 Kings 6:24-8:15	Acts 7:17-36	Ps. 102:1-7
27-Jun	2 Kings 8:16-9:37	Acts 7:37-53	Ps. 102:8-17
28-Jun	2 Kings 10-11	Acts 7:54-8:8	Ps. 102:18-28
29-Jun	2 Kings 12-13	Acts 8:9-40	Ps. 103:1-9
30-Jun	2 Kings 14-15	Acts 9:1-16	Ps. 103:10-14
1-Jul	2 Kings 16-17	Acts 9:17-31	Ps. 103:15-22
2-Jul	2 Kings 18:1-19:7	Acts 9:32-10:16	Ps. 104:1-9
3-Jul	2 Kings 19:8-20:21	Acts 10:17-33	Ps. 104:10-23
4-Jul	2 Kings 21:1-22:20	Acts 10:34-11:18	Ps. 104: 24-30
5-Jul	2 Kings 23	Acts 11:19-12:17	Ps. 104:31-35
6-Jul	2 Kings 24-25	Acts 12:18-13:13	Ps. 105:1-7
7-Jul	1 Chron. 1-2	Acts 13:14-43	Ps. 105:8-15
8-Jul	1 Chron. 3:1-5:10	Acts 13:44-14:10	Ps. 105:16-28
9-Jul	1 Chron. 5:11-6:81	Acts 14:11-28	Ps. 105:29-36
10-Jul	1 Chron. 7:1-9:9	Acts 15:1-18	Ps. 105:37-45
11-Jul	1 Chron. 9:10-11:9	Acts 15:19-41	Ps. 106:1-12
12-Jul	1 Chron. 11:10-12:40	Acts 16:1-15	Ps. 106:13-27
13-Jul	1 Chron. 13-15	Acts 16:16-40	Ps. 106:28-33
14-Jul	1 Chron. 16-17	Acts 17:1-14	Ps. 106:34-43
15-Jul	1 Chron. 18-20	Acts 17:15-34	Ps. 106:44-48
16-Jul	1 Chron. 21-22	Acts 18:1-23	Ps. 107:1-9
17-Jul	1 Chron. 23-25	Acts 18:24-19:10	Ps. 107:10-16
18-Jul	1 Chron. 26-27	Acts 19:11-22	Ps. 107:17-32
19-Jul	1 Chron. 28-29	Acts 19:23-41	Ps. 107:33-38
20-Jul	2 Chron. 1-3	Acts 20:1-16	Ps. 107:39-43
21-Jul	2 Chron. 4:1-6:11	Acts 20:17-38	Ps. 108
22-Jul	2 Chron. 6:12-7:10	Acts 21:1-14	Ps. 109:1-20
23-Jul	2 Chron. 7:11-9:28	Acts 21:15-32	Ps. 109:21-31
24-Jul	2 Chron. 9:29-12:16	Acts 21:33-22:16	Ps. 110:1-3
25-Jul	2 Chron. 13-15	Acts 22:17-23:11	Ps. 110:4-7
26-Jul	2 Chron. 16-17	Acts 23:12-24:21	Ps. 111
27-Jul	2 Chron. 18-19	Acts 24:22-25:12	Ps. 112
28-Jul	2 Chron. 20-21	Acts 25:13-27	Ps. 113

29-Jul	2 Chron. 22-23	Acts 26	Ps. 114
30-Jul	2 Chron. 24:1-25:16	Acts 27:1-20	Ps. 115:1-10
31-Jul	2 Chron. 25:17-27:9	Acts 27:21-28:6	Ps. 115:11-18
1-Aug	2 Chron. 28:1-29:19	Acts 28:7-31	Ps. 116:1-5
2-Aug	2 Chron. 29:20-30:27	Rom. 1:1-17	Ps. 116:6-19
3-Aug	2 Chron. 31-32	Rom. 1:18-32	Ps. 117
4-Aug	2 Chron. 33:1-34:7	Rom. 2	Ps. 118:1-18
5-Aug	2 Chron. 34:8-35:19	Rom. 3:1-26	Ps. 118:19-23
6-Aug	2 Chron. 35:20-36:23	Rom. 3:27-4:25	Ps. 118:24-29
7-Aug	Ezra 1-3	Rom. 5	Ps. 119:1-8
8-Aug	Ezra 4-5	Rom. 6:1-7:6	Ps. 119:9-16
9-Aug	Ezra 6:1-7:26	Rom. 7:7-25	Ps. 119:17-32
10-Aug	Ezra 7:27-9:4	Rom. 8:1-27	Ps. 119:33-40
11-Aug	Ezra 9:5-10:44	Rom. 8:28-39	Ps. 119:41-64
12-Aug	Neh. 1:1-3:16	Rom. 9:1-18	Ps. 119:65-72
13-Aug	Neh. 3:17-5:13	Rom. 9:19-33	Ps. 119:73-80
14-Aug	Neh. 5:14-7:73	Rom. 10:1-13	Ps. 119:81-88
15-Aug	Neh. 8:1-9:5	Rom. 10:14-11:24	Ps. 119:89-104
16-Aug	Neh. 9:6-10:27	Rom. 11:25-12:8	Ps. 119:105-120
17-Aug	Neh. 10:28-12:26	Rom. 12:9-13:7	Ps. 119:121-128
18-Aug	Neh. 12:27-13:31	Rom. 13:8-14:12	Ps. 119:129-136
19-Aug	Esther 1:1-2:18	Rom. 14:13-15:13	Ps. 119:137-152
20-Aug	Esther 2:19-5:14	Rom. 15:14-21	Ps. 119:153-168
21-Aug	Esther. 6-8	Rom. 15:22-33	Ps. 119:169-176
22-Aug	Esther 9-10	Rom. 16	Ps. 120-122
23-Aug	Job 1-3	1 Cor. 1:1-25	Ps. 123
24-Aug	Job 4-6	1 Cor. 1:26-2:16	Ps. 124-125
25-Aug	Job 7-9	1 Cor. 3	Ps. 126-127
26-Aug	Job 10-13	1 Cor. 4:1-13	Ps. 128-129
27-Aug	Job 14-16	1 Cor. 4:14-5:13	Ps. 130
28-Aug	Job 17-20	1 Cor. 6	Ps. 131
29-Aug	Job 21-23	1 Cor. 7:1-16	Ps. 132
30-Aug	Job 24-27	1 Cor. 7:17-40	Ps. 133-134
31-Aug	Job 28-30	1 Cor. 8	Ps. 135
1-Sep	Job 31-33	1 Cor. 9:1-18	Ps. 136:1-9
2-Sep	Job 34-36	1 Cor. 9:19-10:13	Ps. 136:10-26
3-Sep	Job 37-39	1 Cor. 10:14-11:1	Ps. 137
4-Sep	Job 40-42	1 Cor. 11:2-34	Ps. 138
5-Sep	Eccles. 1:1-3:15	1 Cor. 12:1-26	Ps. 139:1-6
6-Sep	Eccles. 3:16-6:12	1 Cor. 12:27-13:13	Ps. 139:7-18
7-Sep	Eccles. 7:1-9:12	1 Cor. 14:1-22	Ps. 139:19-24
8-Sep	Eccles. 9:13-12:14	1 Cor. 14:23-15:11	Ps. 140:1-8

9-Sep	SS 1-4	1 Cor. 15:12-34	Ps. 140:9-13
10-Sep	SS 5-8	1 Cor. 15:35-58	Ps. 141
11-Sep	Isa. 1-2	1 Cor. 16	Ps. 142
12-Sep	Isa. 3-5	2 Cor. 1:1-11	Ps. 143:1-6
13-Sep	Isa. 6-8	2 Cor. 1:12-2:4	Ps. 143:7-12
14-Sep	Isa. 9-10	2 Cor. 2:5-17	Ps. 144
15-Sep	Isa. 11-13	2 Cor. 3	Ps. 145
16-Sep	Isa. 14-16	2 Cor. 4	Ps. 146
17-Sep	Isa. 17-19	2 Cor. 5	Ps. 147:1-11
18-Sep	Isa. 20-23	2 Cor. 6	Ps. 147:12-20
19-Sep	Isa. 24:1-26:19	2 Cor. 7	Ps. 148
20-Sep	Isa. 26:20-28:29	2 Cor. 8	Ps. 149-150
21-Sep	Isa. 29-30	2 Cor. 9	Prov. 1:1-9
22-Sep	Isa. 31-33	2 Cor. 10	Prov. 1:10-22
23-Sep	Isa. 34-36	2 Cor. 11	Prov. 1:23-26
24-Sep	Isa. 37-38	2 Cor. 12:1-10	Prov. 1:27-33
25-Sep	Isa. 39-40	2 Cor. 12:11-13:14	Prov. 2:1-15
26-Sep	Isa. 41-42	Gal. 1	Prov. 2:16-22
27-Sep	Isa. 43:1-44:20	Gal. 2	Prov. 3:1-12
28-Sep	Isa. 44:21-46:13	Gal. 3:1-18	Prov. 3:13-26
29-Sep	Isa. 47:1-49:13	Gal 3:19-29	Prov. 3:27-35
30-Sep	Isa. 49:14-51:23	Gal 4:1-11	Prov. 4:1-19
1-Oct	Isa. 52-54	Gal. 4:12-31	Prov. 4:20-27
2-Oct	Isa. 55-57	Gal. 5	Prov. 5:1-14
3-Oct	Isa. 58-59	Gal. 6	Prov. 5:15-23
4-Oct	Isa. 60-62	Eph. 1	Prov. 6:1-5
5-Oct	Isa. 63:1-65:16	Eph. 2	Prov. 6:6-19
6-Oct	Isa. 65:17-66:24	Eph. 3:1-4:16	Prov. 6:20-26
7-Oct	Jer. 1-2	Eph. 4:17-32	Prov. 6:27-35
8-Oct	Jer. 3:1-4:22	Eph. 5	Prov. 7:1-5
9-Oct	Jer. 4:23-5:31	Eph. 6	Prov. 7:6-27
10-Oct	Jer. 6:1-7:26	Phil. 1:1-26	Prov. 8:1-11
11-Oct	Jer. 7:26-9:16	Phil. 1:27-2:18	Prov. 8:12-21
12-Oct	Jer. 9:17-11:17	Phil 2:19-30	Prov. 8:22-36
13-Oct	Jer. 11:18-13:27	Phil. 3	Prov. 9:1-6
14-Oct	Jer. 14-15	Phil. 4	Prov. 9:7-18
15-Oct	Jer. 16-17	Col. 1:1-23	Prov. 10:1-5
16-Oct	Jer. 18:1-20:6	Col. 1:24-2:15	Prov. 10:6-14
17-Oct	Jer. 20:7-22:19	Col. 2:16-3:4	Prov. 10:15-26
18-Oct	Jer. 22:20-23:40	Col. 3:5-4:1	Prov. 10:27-32
19-Oct	Jer. 24-25	Col. 4:2-18	Prov. 11:1-11
20-Oct	Jer. 26-27	1 Thes. 1:1-2:8	Prov. 11:12-21

21-Oct	Jer. 28-29	1 Thes. 2:9-3:13	Prov. 11:22-26
22-Oct	Jer. 30:1-31:22	1 Thes. 4:1-5:11	Prov. 11:27-31
23-Oct	Jer. 31:23-32:35	1 Thes. 5:12-28	Prov. 12:1-14
24-Oct	Jer. 32:36-34:7	2 Thes. 1-2	Prov. 12:15-20
25-Oct	Jer. 34:8-36:10	2 Thes. 3	Prov. 12:21-28
26-Oct	Jer. 36:11-38:13	1 Tim. 1:1-17	Prov. 13:1-4
27-Oct	Jer. 38:14-40:6	1 Tim. 1:18-3:13	Prov. 13:5-13
28-Oct	Jer. 40:7-42:22	1 Tim. 3:14-4:10	Prov. 13:14-21
29-Oct	Jer. 43-44	1 Tim. 4:11-5:16	Prov. 13:22-25
30-Oct	Jer. 45-47	1 Tim. 5:17-6:21	Prov. 14:1-6
31-Oct	Jer. 48:1-49:6	2 Tim. 1	Prov. 14:7-22
1-Nov	Jer. 49:7-50:16	2 Tim. 2	Prov. 14:23-27
2-Nov	Jer. 50:17-51:14	2 Tim. 3	Prov. 14:28-35
3-Nov	Jer. 51:15-64	2 Tim. 4	Prov. 15:1-9
4-Nov	Jer. 52-Lam. 1	Ti. 1:1-9	Prov. 15:10-17
5-Nov	Lam. 2:1-3:38	Ti. 1:10-2:15	Prov. 15:18-26
6-Nov	Lam. 3:39-5:22	Ti. 3	Prov. 15:27-33
7-Nov	Ezek. 1:1-3:21	Philemon 1	Prov. 16:1-9
8-Nov	Ezek. 3:22-5:17	Heb. 1:1-2:4	Prov. 16:10-21
9-Nov	Ezek. 6-7	Heb. 2:5-18	Prov. 16:22-33
10-Nov	Ezek. 8-10	Heb. 3:1-4:3	Prov. 17:1-5
11-Nov	Ezek. 11-12	Heb. 4:4-5:10	Prov. 17:6-12
12-Nov	Ezek. 13-14	Heb. 5:11-6:20	Prov. 17:13-22
13-Nov	Ezek. 15:1-16:43	Heb. 7:1-28	Prov. 17:23-28
14-Nov	Ezek. 16:44-17:24	Heb. 8:1-9:10	Prov. 18:1-7
15-Nov	Ezek. 18-19	Heb. 9:11-28	Prov. 18:8-17
16-Nov	Ezek. 20	Heb. 10:1-25	Prov. 18:18-24
17-Nov	Ezek. 21-22	Heb. 10:26-39	Prov. 19:1-8
18-Nov	Ezek. 23	Heb. 11:1-31	Prov. 19:9-14
19-Nov	Ezek. 24-26	Heb. 11:32-40	Prov. 19:15-21
20-Nov	Ezek. 27-28	Heb. 12:1-13	Prov. 19:22-29
21-Nov	Ezek. 29-30	Heb. 12:14-29	Prov. 20:1-18
22-Nov	Ezek. 31-32	Heb. 13	Prov. 20:19-24
23-Nov	Ezek. 33:1-34:10	Jas. 1	Prov. 20:25-30
24-Nov	Ezek. 34:11-36:15	Jas. 2	Prov. 21:1-8
25-Nov	Ezek. 36:16-37:28	Jas. 3	Prov. 21:9-18
26-Nov	Ezek. 38-39	Jas. 4:1-5:6	Prov. 21:19-24
27-Nov	Ezek. 40	Jas. 5:7-20	Prov. 21:25-31
28-Nov	Ezek. 41:1-43:12	1 Pet. 1:1-12	Prov. 22:1-9
29-Nov	Ezek. 43:13-44:31	1 Pet. 1:13-2:3	Prov. 22:10-23
30-Nov	Ezek. 45-46	1 Pet. 2:4-17	Prov. 22:24-29
1-Dec	Ezek. 47-48	1 Pet. 2:18-3:7	Prov. 23:1-9

2-Dec	Dan. 1:1-2:23	1 Pet. 3:8-4:19	Prov. 23:10-16
3-Dec	Dan. 2:24-3:30	1 Pet. 5	Prov. 23:17-25
4-Dec	Dan. 4	2 Pet. 1	Prov. 23:26-35
5-Dec	Dan. 5	2 Pet. 2	Prov. 24:1-18
6-Dec	Dan. 6:1-7:14	2 Pet. 3	Prov. 24:19-27
7-Dec	Dan. 7:15-8:27	1 John 1:1-2:17	Prov. 24:28-34
8-Dec	Dan. 9-10	1 John 2:18-29	Prov. 25:1-12
9-Dec	Dan. 11-12	1 John 3:1-12	Prov. 25:13-17
10-Dec	Hos. 1-3	1 John 3:13-4:16	Prov. 25:18-28
11-Dec	Hos. 4-6	1 John 4:17-5:21	Prov. 26:1-16
12-Dec	Hos. 7-10	2 John	Prov. 26:17-21
13-Dec	Hos. 11-14	3 John	Prov. 26:22-27:9
14-Dec	Joel 1:1-2:17	Jude	Prov. 27:10-17
15-Dec	Joel 2:18-3:21	Rev. 1:1-2:11	Prov. 27:18-27
16-Dec	Amos 1:1-4:5	Rev. 2:12-29	Prov. 28:1-8
17-Dec	Amos 4:6-6:14	Rev. 3	Prov. 28:9-16
18-Dec	Amos 7-9	Rev. 4:1-5:5	Prov. 28:17-24
19-Dec	Obad-Jonah	Rev. 5:6-14	Prov. 28:25-28
20-Dec	Mic. 1:1-4:5	Rev. 6:1-7:8	Prov. 29:1-8
21-Dec	Mic. 4:6-7:20	Rev. 7:9-8:13	Prov. 29:9-14
22-Dec	Nah. 1-3	Rev. 9-10	Prov. 29:15-23
23-Dec	Hab. 1-3	Rev. 11	Prov. 29:24-27
24-Dec	Zeph. 1-3	Rev. 12	Prov. 30:1-6
25-Dec	Hag. 1-2	Rev. 13:1-14:13	Prov. 30:7-16
26-Dec	Zech. 1-4	Rev. 14:14-16:3	Prov. 30:17-20
27-Dec	Zech. 5-8	Rev. 16:4-21	Prov. 30:21-28
28-Dec	Zech. 9-11	Rev. 17:1-18:8	Prov. 30:29-33
29-Dec	Zech. 12-14	Rev. 18:9-24	Prov. 31:1-9
30-Dec	Mal. 1-2	Rev. 19-20	Prov. 31:10-17
31-Dec	Mal. 3-4	Rev. 21-22	Prov. 31:18-31